PRECIOUS MOMENTS

IN PLASTIC CANVAS

Imagine the fun you can have combining the adorable appeal of PRECIOUS MOMENTS® characters with the versatility of plastic canvas! This big book of Precious Moments in Plastic Canvas *offers exclusive designs featuring characters inspired by Sam Butcher's irresistible innocents. Among the world's most sought-after collectibles, the cherished children are ideal for decorating and accessorizing your home and creating memorable gifts. Our must-have treasury contains a large variety of one-of-a-kind, top-quality PRECIOUS MOMENTS designs — from fun items like Tooth Fairy baskets, a pretty purse, and adorable magnets to beautiful door decorations, pictures, and frames. You can mark special occasions such as weddings and graduations with winsome photo album covers and charm your friends or a favorite teacher with tissue box covers, a recipe set, or a handmade rug. Whether you're adding to a PRECIOUS MOMENTS collection or just starting out, you'll love these sentimental creations!*

LEISURE ARTS, INC.
and
OXMOOR HOUSE, INC.

IN PLASTIC CANVAS

EDITORIAL STAFF

Vice President and Editor-in-Chief:
Anne Van Wagner Childs
Executive Director: Sandra Graham Case
Executive Director: Susan Frantz Wiles
Publications Director: Carla Bentley
Creative Art Director: Gloria Bearden
Senior Graphics Art Director: Melinda Stout

PRODUCTION
Senior Publications Editor: Sherry Taylor O'Connor
Senior Special Projects Editor: Donna Brown Hill
Special Projects Editor: Connie White Irby
Project Coordinators: Andrea Ahlen, Emily Ford,
Catherine Hubmann, Mary Sullivan Hutcheson,
Sherry James, Susan McManus Johnson,
Lisa Hinkle Lancaster, Beth M. Maher, and
Tracy Cansler Thomas
Project Assistants: Lylln Craig, JoAnn Forrest,
and Janie Wright

EDITORIAL
Managing Editor: Linda L. Trimble
Associate Editor: Janice Teipen Wojcik
Editorial Associates: Tammi Williamson Bradley
and Terri Leming Davidson
Copy Editor: Laura Lee Weland

DESIGN
Design Director: Patricia Wallenfang Sowers

ART
Crafts Art Director: Rhonda Hodge Shelby
Senior Production Artist: Mary Ellen Wilhelm
Production Artists: Sonya McFatrich, Keith Melton,
Brent Miller, Katie Murphy, Dana Vaughn,
and Karen L. Wilson
Photography Stylists: Beth Carter, Pam Choate,
Aurora Huston, and Laura Dell Reed

PROMOTIONS
Managing Editors: Tena Kelley Vaughn and
Marjorie Ann Lacy
Associate Editors: Steven M. Cooper, Dixie L. Morris,
and Jennifer Leigh Ertl
Designer: Dale Rowett
Art Director: Linda Lovette Smart
Production Artist: Leslie Loring Krebs
Publishing Systems Administrator: Cindy Lumpkin
Publishing Systems Assistant: Susan Mary Gray

BUSINESS STAFF

Publisher: Bruce Akin
Vice President, Marketing: Guy A. Crossley
Marketing Manager: Byron L. Taylor
Print Production Manager: Laura Lockhart
Vice President and General Manager:
Thomas L. Carlisle
Retail Sales Director: Richard Tignor

Vice President, Retail Marketing: Pam Stebbins
Retail Marketing Director: Margaret Sweetin
Retail Customer Services Manager: Carolyn Pruss
General Merchandise Manager: Russ Barnett
Vice President, Finance: Tom Siebenmorgen
Distribution Director: Ed M. Strackbein

PRECIOUS MOMENTS IN PLASTIC CANVAS
from the *Plastic Canvas Creations* series
Published by Leisure Arts, Inc., and Oxmoor House, Inc.

Library of Congress Catalog Number 97-73651
Hardcover ISBN 0-8487-4161-7
Softcover ISBN 1-57486-051-8

©1997 Precious Moments, Inc.

TABLE OF CONTENTS

Bouquet Cover-up

A wistful young lady holding a just-picked flower adorns this happy-go-lucky tissue box cover. The little miss is worked on 10 mesh canvas with pastel sport weight yarn.

Instructions on page 38

Cute Kitchen Collection

These pieces make a wonderful kitchen collection for your favorite food fanatic! Our petite chef's helper graces a recipe box and bookend designed to hold the best-ever cookbooks and recipes. There's even a nifty napkin holder! If you can bear to part with this charming set, make your gift more endearing by including favorite family recipes or an extra-special cookbook.

Instructions on page 35

Instructions
on page 40

"God's Workmanship" Wreath

The soft pastels of a spring garden are tastefully offset by the rustic beauty of this grapevine wreath, which will quickly find a perfect perch in your home or that of a friend. Our little miss is worked on 10 mesh canvas with sport weight yarn.

Pretty Pocketbook

Whether she's going shopping, out to eat, or to Sunday school, your little princess will carry her most valued treasures in this pretty purse. Scaled to her size, the petite pocketbook is worked on 7 mesh canvas with the girl in 10 mesh.

Instructions on page 41

Baby Boy With Blocks

With an irresistible smile, tousled hair, and a perky turned-up nose, our blissful baby perches atop a group of colorful building blocks. Clever placement of the youngster's arms and legs achieves a three-dimensional effect that adds to his animated appearance.

Instructions on page 44

Charming Totes

These tote bags are keepers — for your Bible study needs, your stitching supplies, and more! Or you can pack a lunch and the newspaper in these winsome reminders of the innocence of childhood. Versatile as well as charming, the totes also make nice gift bags that are gifts in themselves.

Instructions on page 47

Humble Holy Family

Beneath the twinkle of a brightly shining star, the Holy Family rests serenely in a humble stable. This Nativity scene will add a touch of holiness to any corner of your home. The characters are worked on 10 mesh canvas with sport weight yarn; the manger and star are 7 mesh canvas with worsted weight yarn.

Instructions on page 65

Terrific Teacher Tissue Cover

This heartwarming tissue box cover will thank an extra-special teacher for "going the extra mile" by presenting the ABC's in an atmosphere of loving, caring, and sharing! This practical item is worked entirely on 10 mesh canvas with sport weight yarn.

Instructions on page 50

Endearing Yuletide Banner

Two fundamental Christmas ingredients — children and tree-trimming — are brought together in this fetching Yuletide banner. Perfect for the mantel, wall, or door, this unique accent uses 10 mesh canvas for the children and tree and 7 mesh for the background.

Instructions on page 52

Delightful Magnets

Our brown-eyed boy and his delightful blonde companions make eye-catching magnets for posting telephone messages, shopping lists, and outstanding report cards. The easy-to-stitch designs are worked on 10 mesh canvas with sport weight yarn.

Bible Study
Picnic
Sun. 4:00

Instructions on page 41

Treasure Box

*Our "a-lure-ing" treasure box depicts a beautiful backdrop for a day of fishing —
a vibrant blue sky with a white, fluffy cloud floating past. This unique container
provides a handy place to store items prized by the young — or young at heart.*

Instructions on page 54

Bedtime Prayers

Freshly bathed and ready for bedtime blessings, our prayerful children kneel for their end-of-day ritual. This duo of heart-stealers is equally charming for the guest room, family room, or nursery.

Instructions on page 56

friends Are forever Rug

Whether we're 8 or 80, our friends are an enduring joy. Your forever friend will have a sweet reminder of your thoughtfulness and love when you give this precious rug, which is worked on 5 mesh canvas with two strands of worsted weight yarn.

Instructions on page 90

Rainy Day Bank

Toss your loose change into this cute Rainy Day Bank and watch the money add up! Then, when a dark and dreary day comes to cloud your world, you can beat the blues with an extraordinary treat. This bank is also a perfect place for stashing the cash you save when using coupons. Ten mesh canvas is used for the young miss, with 7 mesh canvas for the bank.

Instructions on page 58

Lovely Wreath

Bestow a refreshing breath of springtime on any niche in your house with this lovely wreath. The soft pastels of our young miss and her blossoms are echoed in the floral accents that enhance the willow wreath.

Instructions on page 38

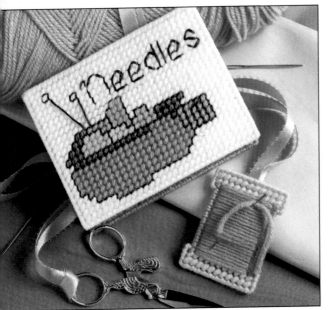

A Stitch In Time Sewing Set

A stitch in time from our motherly seamstress mends the wear-and-tear on our little cherub's wings. This heartwarming scene graces the cover of a sewing box large enough to hold all the basic stitching necessities — and then some! To complete the set, there's a nifty needle case and a beribboned chatelaine anchored with your favorite scissors and a spool-shaped pin-holder.

Instructions on page 60

Blissful Wedding Day Ensemble

The cherubic figures adorning this photo album cover and centerpiece capture the pomp and ceremony of a formal wedding in a delightfully innocent manner. Worked on white 10 mesh canvas, the design is highlighted with metallic yarn, which adds a pretty sheen to the bridal veil. The candy-filled favors feature a charming heart motif.

Instructions on page 62

20

Instructions on page 62

Tooth Fairy Baskets

What a clever idea! No more fears and tears because a misplaced tooth disappears before the Tooth Fairy can perform her magic. Worked in sport weight yarn on 10 mesh canvas, these containers make darling shelf decorations when not holding teeny teeth.

GOD BLESS THE TOOTH FAIRY

GOD BLESS THE TOOTH FAIRY

Instructions on page 56

Bathing Beauty

Scrub a dub dub, this little lady's surrounded by luxurious bubbles!
Metallic yarn makes the floating bubbles sparkle on this charming 10 mesh piece.

Instructions on page 68

Graduation Photo Albums

*These quick-and-easy album toppers capture the hopefulness and wonder of graduation.
The designs are stitched on 10 mesh canvas and then glued onto snapshot albums.
You can use the graduates' school colors for the embroidery-floss tassels.*

Instructions on page 70

Blessed Bookends

*Charming as bookends or doorstops, these prayerful children
kneel in colorful flower beds. The humble duo inspires us to
stop and give thanks in the midst of our fast-paced lives.*

Instructions on page 78

Princely Desk Set

Make that special man in the house feel like a king with these desk accessories!
He can organize office necessities — such as books, files, pencils, and paper clips —
under the watchful eye of our friendly young prince, who is worked on 10 mesh canvas.

Instructions on page 72

"Jesus Loves Me" Frame

A lovable bear and bunny hold a heart-shaped picture frame just waiting for a photo of your precious darling. The verse is a ready reminder that every loved one, whether newborn or up in years, is a gift from heaven.

Instructions on page 74

Heavenly Inspiration

One look at our inspirational angels will chase away the Monday blues or the Wednesday blahs! In this heavenly 10 mesh design, the mischievous cherubs are resting on Cloud 9 with their halos perfectly in place.

Instructions on page 76

Captivating Coasters

Sipping refreshing lemonade on the patio or a satisfying soda in the family room is a relaxing diversion. Using 10 mesh coasters featuring our terrific trio will add to the enjoyment of quenching your thirst.

Instructions on page 41

Country Friends Bookends

Your most cherished books will be lovingly nestled between these bookends, which capture the appeal of two lovable children with a graceful goose and a cuddly chick on 10 mesh canvas. The stands are ordinary metal bookends that take on a cozy appearance with 7 mesh plastic canvas "slipcovers."

Instructions on page 81

Perky Door Decoration

Take a fresh approach to greeting your guests with this perky door decoration. From her straw skimmer to the colorful bows in her hair, our little lady exudes charm and innocence. Use two strands of worsted weight yarn to work this design on 5 mesh canvas.

Instructions on page 84

Winsome Door Hangers

Featuring a gallant guardian angel or a bashful bunny lover, our winsome charmers remind visitors that a special someone dwells behind the doors they adorn.

Instructions on pages 86 and 87

Sweet Dreams Wall Hanging

An angelic child slumbers in a billowing cloud surrounded by hearts, flowers, and a perky bluebird on our sweet wall decoration. This serene scene, worked with two strands of worsted weight yarn on 5 mesh canvas, is a nice touch for the nursery.

Instructions on page 88

33

OUR PRECIOUS PALETTE

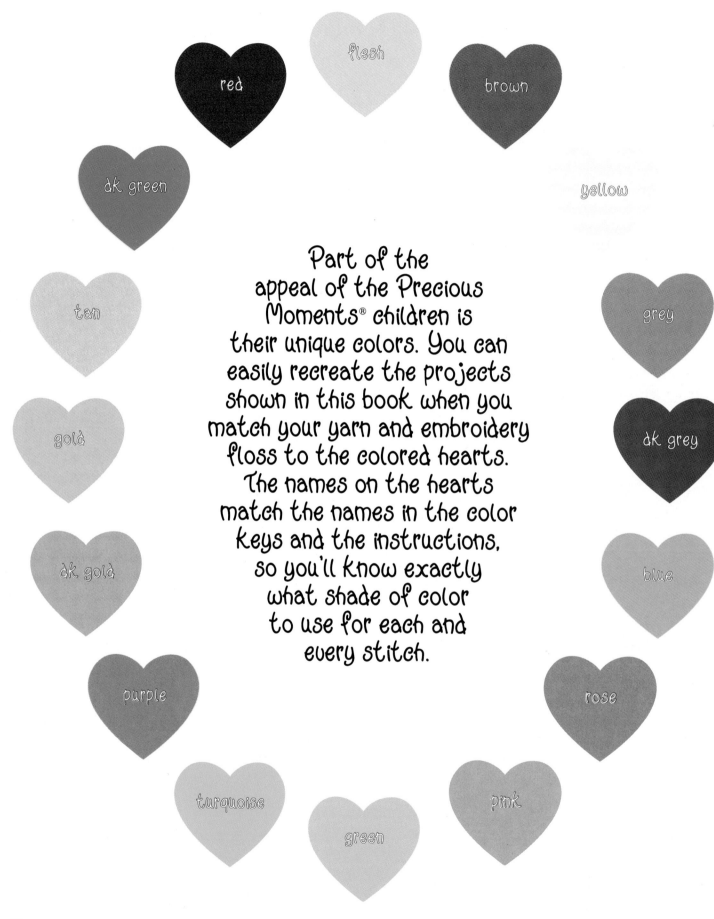

red

flesh

brown

dk green

yellow

tan

grey

gold

dk grey

Part of the
appeal of the Precious
Moments® children is
their unique colors. You can
easily recreate the projects
shown in this book when you
match your yarn and embroidery
floss to the colored hearts.
The names on the hearts
match the names in the color
keys and the instructions,
so you'll know exactly
what shade of color
to use for each and
every stitch.

dk gold

blue

purple

rose

turquoise

green

pink

Cute Kitchen Collection
(Shown on page 5)

Napkin Holder Size: 7½"w x 7"h x 2¾"d
Recipe Box Size: 6¼"w x 3¾"h x 4½"d
Bookend Size: 4¾"w x 10¼"h x 2¾"d
Supplies: Worsted weight yarn, sport weight yarn, embroidery floss, four 10½" x 13½" sheets of clear 7 mesh stiff plastic canvas, one 10½" x 13½" sheet of white 7 mesh plastic canvas, one 10½" x 13½" sheet of white 10 mesh plastic canvas, #16 tapestry needle, #20 tapestry needle, 3½"w x 7½"h x 2⅛"d brick, plastic wrap, and craft glue
Stitches Used: Backstitch, French Knot, Gobelin Stitch, Overcast Stitch, Scotch Stitch, and Tent Stitch
Napkin Holder Instructions: Follow chart to cut and stitch Chef on white 10 mesh plastic canvas. Follow charts to cut and stitch remaining Napkin Holder pieces on clear 7 mesh plastic canvas.
Using blue yarn, join Sides to Front. Join Back to Sides. For Bottom, cut a piece of clear 7 mesh plastic canvas 49 x 18 threads. (**Note:** Bottom is not worked.) Join Bottom to Front, Back, and Sides. Glue Chef to Front.

Recipe Box Instructions: Follow chart to cut and stitch Chef head and neck only on white 10 mesh plastic canvas. Follow charts to cut and stitch remaining Recipe Box pieces on clear 7 mesh plastic canvas.
For Recipe Box Top, join long unworked edges of Side #1 pieces to long edges of Top using blue yarn. Join long unworked edges of Side #2 pieces to short edges of Top. Join Side pieces together using white yarn.
For Recipe Box, match short edges and join Front to Sides using blue yarn. Join Back to Sides. For Bottom, cut a piece of clear 7 mesh plastic canvas 38 x 26 threads. (**Note:** Bottom is not worked.) Join Bottom to Front, Back, and Sides. Glue Chef to Top.

Bookend Instructions: Follow chart to cut and stitch Chef on white 7 mesh plastic canvas. Refer to page 80 to cut and stitch Back, Top, Bottom, and Side pieces on clear 7 mesh plastic canvas using blue yarn. For Front, cut a piece of canvas 27 x 56 threads and stitch following the Back chart.
Using blue yarn, match long edges and join Front to Sides. Join Back to Sides. Join Top to Front, Back, and Sides. Wrap plastic wrap around brick and insert brick into Bookend. Join Bottom to Front, Back, and Sides. Glue Chef to Bookend.

WORSTED WEIGHT YARN	
⁄	white
⁄	blue
⁄	green
•	pink French Knot

Napkin Holder Side

(18 x 23 threads) (stitch 2) 7 mesh

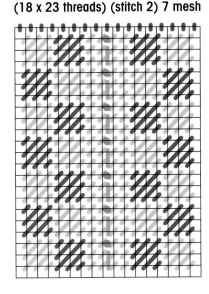

Napkin Holder Front/Back (49 x 35 threads) (stitch 2) 7 mesh

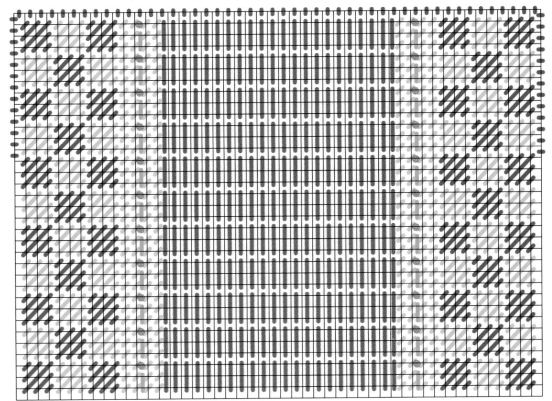

Continued on page 36

WORSTED WEIGHT YARN

- ⟋ white
- ⟋ blue
- ⟋ green
- ● pink French Knot

EMBROIDERY FLOSS

- ⟋ dk grey - 6 strands

Recipe Box Top Side #1 (41 x 7 threads) (stitch 2) 7 mesh

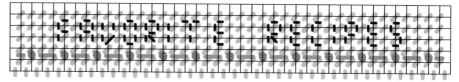

Recipe Box Top Side #2 (29 x 7 threads) (stitch 2) 7 mesh

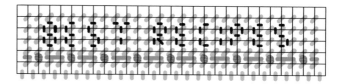

Recipe Box Top (41 x 29 threads) 7 mesh

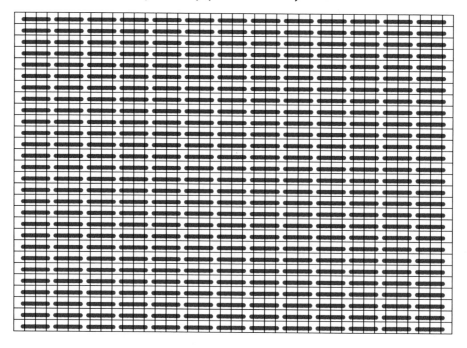

Recipe Box Side
(26 x 23 threads) (stitch 2) 7 mesh

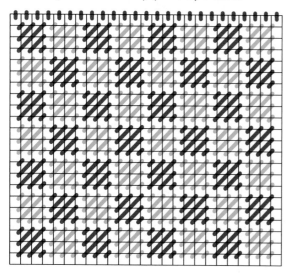

Recipe Box Front/Back
(38 x 23 threads) (stitch 2) 7 mesh

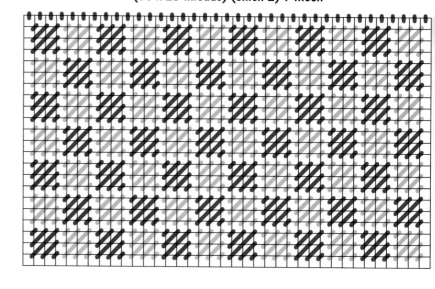

SPORT WEIGHT YARN

- ⟋ white
- ⟋ yellow
- ⟋ flesh
- ⟋ pink
- ⟋ blue
- ⟋ green
- ⟋ brown
- ⟋ dk grey
- ⊙ yellow French Knot
- ◉ pink French Knot
- ● blue French Knot

EMBROIDERY FLOSS

- ⟋ * dk grey
- ⟋ † dk grey
- ● * white French Knot

* For 10 mesh canvas, use
1 strand of floss. For 7 mesh
canvas, use 3 strands of floss.

† For 10 mesh canvas, use
2 strands of floss. For 7 mesh
canvas, use 6 strands of floss.

Chef (34 x 69 threads)

Stitch to this thread
for Recipe Box.

Bouquet Cover-up

(Shown on page 4)
Size: 4³/₄"w x 7³/₄"h x 5"d
(Fits a 4¹/₄"w x 5³/₈"h x 4¹/₄"d boutique tissue box.)
Supplies: Worsted weight yarn, sport weight yarn, embroidery floss, two 10¹/₂" x 13¹/₂" sheets of clear 7 mesh plastic canvas, one 10¹/₂" x 13¹/₂" sheet of white 10 mesh plastic canvas, #16 tapestry needle, #20 tapestry needle, and craft glue
Stitches Used: Alternating Scotch Stitch, Backstitch, French Knot, Gobelin Stitch, Overcast Stitch, and Tent Stitch
Instructions: Follow chart to cut and stitch Girl on 10 mesh plastic canvas. Follow charts to cut and stitch remaining tissue box cover pieces on 7 mesh plastic canvas.
Using matching color yarn, match long edges and join Front to Sides. Join Back to Sides. Using white yarn, join Top to Front, Back, and Sides. Glue Girl to tissue box cover.

Lovely Wreath

(Shown on page 18)
Girl Size: 7¹/₄"w x 11³/₄"h
Wreath Size: 16" dia
Supplies: Worsted weight yarn, embroidery floss, one 10¹/₂" x 13¹/₂" sheet of white 7 mesh plastic canvas, #16 tapestry needle, 16" dia willow wreath, assorted flowers and greenery, two yds of 1¹/₂"w wire-edge ribbon, two yds of 1¹/₂"w sheer ribbon, and craft glue
Stitches Used: Backstitch, French Knot, and Tent Stitch
Instructions: Follow chart to cut and stitch Girl. Glue flowers to wreath. Tie ribbons into a bow and trim ends. Glue bow to wreath. Glue Girl to wreath.

WORSTED WEIGHT YARN	
⧄	white
⧄	blue
⦿	blue French Knot

Top (32 x 32 threads) 7 mesh

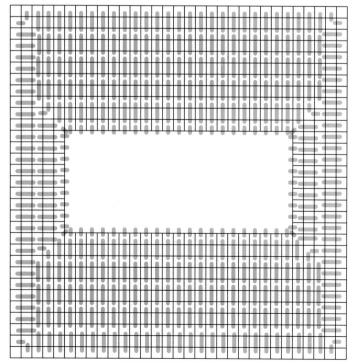

Front/Back (32 x 37 threads) (stitch 2) 7 mesh

Side (32 x 37 threads) (stitch 2) 7 mesh

Girl (48 x 78 threads)

SPORT WEIGHT YARN
- white
- flesh
- pink
- rose
- purple
- blue
- green
- tan
- dk grey
- white French Knot

EMBROIDERY FLOSS
- * dk grey
- † dk grey
- * white French Knot

* For 10 mesh canvas, use
  1 strand of floss. For 7 mesh
  canvas, use 3 strands of floss.
† For 10 mesh canvas, use
  2 strands of floss. For 7 mesh
  canvas, use 6 strands of floss.

"God's Workmanship" Wreath

(Shown on page 6)

Girl Size: 4¼"w x 8½"h

Wreath Size: 15" dia

Supplies: Sport weight yarn, embroidery floss, one 10½" x 13½" sheet of white 10 mesh plastic canvas, #20 tapestry needle, 15" dia wreath, assorted flowers and greenery, two yds of 1½"w wire-edge ribbon, and craft glue

Stitches Used: Backstitch, French Knot, and Tent Stitch

Instructions: Follow chart to cut and stitch Girl. Glue flowers to wreath. Tie ribbon into a bow and trim ends. Glue bow to wreath. Glue Girl to wreath.

Girl (43 x 87 threads)

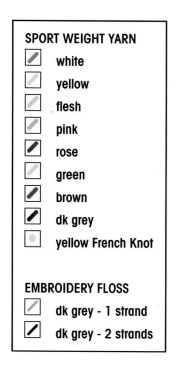

SPORT WEIGHT YARN

- white
- yellow
- flesh
- pink
- rose
- green
- brown
- dk grey
- yellow French Knot

EMBROIDERY FLOSS

- dk grey - 1 strand
- dk grey - 2 strands

Pretty Pocketbook

(Shown on page 7)

Size: 5¼"w x 10¾"h x 2¼"d

Supplies: Worsted weight yarn, sport weight yarn, embroidery floss, one 10½" x 13½" sheet of white 7 mesh plastic canvas, one 10½" x 13½" sheet of white 10 mesh plastic canvas, #16 tapestry needle, #20 tapestry needle, ¾"w x 1"l Velcro® brand fastener, sewing needle and thread, and craft glue

Stitches Used: Backstitch, Cross Stitch, French Knot, Gobelin Stitch, Overcast Stitch, and Tent Stitch

Instructions: Follow chart to cut Girl #2 from 10 mesh plastic canvas along green cutting lines. Follow chart to stitch design. Follow charts to cut and stitch Purse pieces on 7 mesh plastic canvas. Using white yarn, join Front to Sides. With wrong sides facing inward, work stitches in shaded areas to join Back to Sides. Join Bottom to Front, Back, and Sides. Join Handle to Sides. Using sewing needle and thread, tack loop (soft) Velcro to wrong side of Back. Tack hook (hard) Velcro to right side of Front. Glue Girl #2 to Purse.

Delightful Magnets

(Shown on page 13)

Approx Size: 3¼"w x 4¾"h each

Supplies: Sport weight yarn, embroidery floss, two 10½" x 13½" sheets of white 10 mesh plastic canvas, #20 tapestry needle, magnetic strip, and craft glue

Stitches Used: Backstitch, French Knot, Overcast Stitch, and Tent Stitch

Instructions: Follow charts to cut canvas along green cutting lines. Follow charts to stitch designs. Glue magnetic strip to back of completed stitched pieces.

Captivating Coasters

(Shown on page 29)

Approx Size: 4½"w x 4¾"h each

Supplies: Sport weight yarn, embroidery floss, two 10½" x 13½" sheets of clear 10 mesh plastic canvas, #20 tapestry needle, cork or felt (optional), and craft glue (optional)

Stitches Used: Backstitch, French Knot, Overcast Stitch, and Tent Stitch

Instructions: Follow charts to cut and stitch pieces. Before adding Backstitches, complete backgrounds with Tent Stitches as indicated on charts and cover unworked edges using matching color yarn. If desired, glue cork or felt to back of completed stitched pieces.

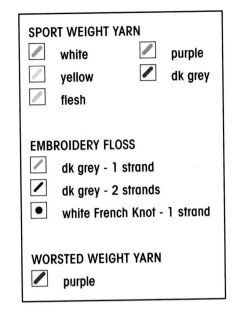

SPORT WEIGHT YARN

	white		purple
	yellow		dk grey
	flesh		

EMBROIDERY FLOSS

dk grey - 1 strand

dk grey - 2 strands

● white French Knot - 1 strand

WORSTED WEIGHT YARN

purple

Purse Bottom
(14 x 32 threads) 7 mesh

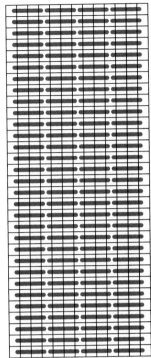

Girl #1 (46 x 51 threads) 10 mesh

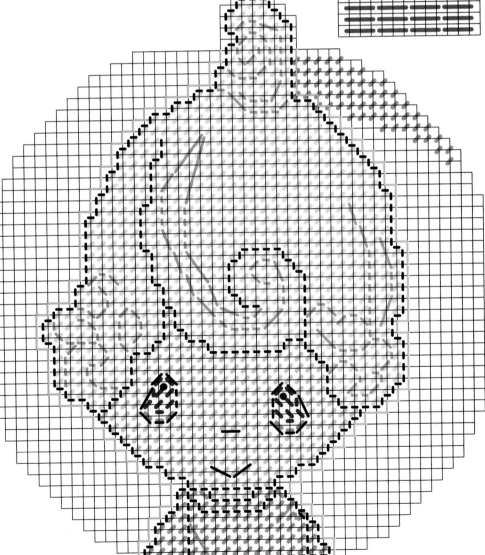

Continued on page 42

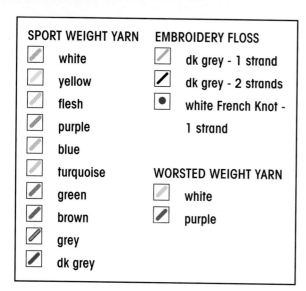
Purse Front (32 x 34 threads) 7 mesh

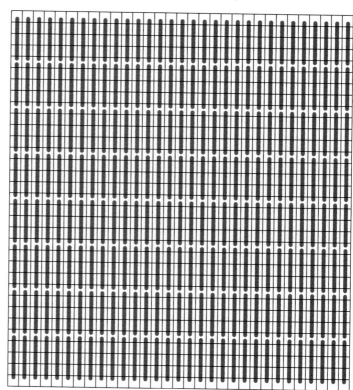

Girl #2 (46 x 47 threads) 10 mesh

Purse Handle

(4 x 90 threads)

7 mesh

Purse Back (82 x 34 threads) 7 mesh

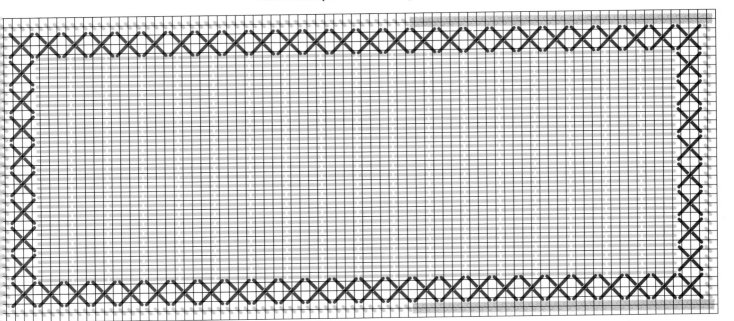

Purse Side (14 x 38 threads)
(stitch 2) 7 mesh

Boy (46 x 46 threads) 10 mesh

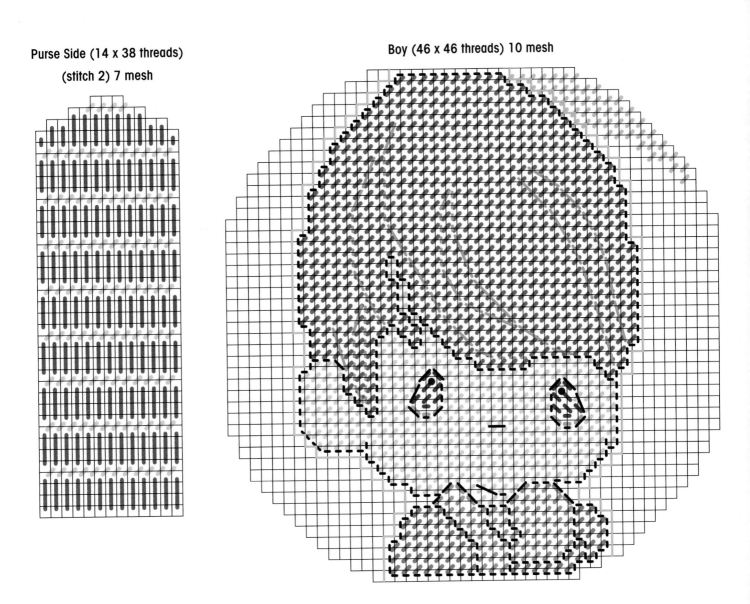

Baby Boy With Blocks

(Shown on page 8)

Baby Size: 9$\frac{1}{4}$"w x 11$\frac{1}{2}$"h x 2$\frac{1}{2}$"d
Block Size: 3$\frac{1}{4}$"w x 3$\frac{1}{4}$"h x 3$\frac{1}{4}$"d each
Small Block Size: 1$\frac{1}{2}$"w x 1$\frac{1}{2}$"h x 1$\frac{1}{2}$"d
Supplies: Worsted weight yarn, embroidery floss, three 10$\frac{1}{2}$" x 13$\frac{1}{2}$" sheets of clear 7 mesh plastic canvas, one 10$\frac{1}{2}$" x 13$\frac{1}{2}$" sheet of white 7 mesh plastic canvas, #16 tapestry needle, sewing needle (for working with nylon thread), nylon thread, two 12" wooden skewers, white paint (optional), and craft glue

Stitches Used: Backstitch, French Knot, Mosaic Stitch, Overcast Stitch, and Tent Stitch

Instructions: Follow charts to cut and stitch Body, Arm, and Leg pieces on white plastic canvas, leaving stitches in shaded areas unworked. Follow charts to cut and stitch remaining pieces on clear canvas. Before adding Backstitches, complete backgrounds of Block pieces with Tent Stitches as indicated on charts.

Matching ■'s and ★'s, work stitches in pink shaded areas to join Right Leg and Left Leg to Body. Matching ♥'s and ✖'s, work stitches in green shaded areas to join Right Arm and Left Arm to Body.

Using matching color yarn, join four Side pieces of "B" Block together to form a square. Using yarn color to match Sides, join Top and Bottom to Sides. Repeat for remaining "A", "B", and "Y" Blocks.

Using matching color yarn, alternate Small Block Side #1 and Side #2 pieces and join together to form a square. Join Top and Bottom to Sides.

If desired, paint wooden skewers. Glue skewers to back of Baby for support. Arrange Blocks as desired. Using nylon line, tack Small Block to Baby. Tack Baby to Blocks.

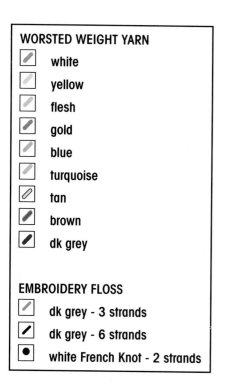

WORSTED WEIGHT YARN

✎	white
✎	yellow
✎	flesh
✎	gold
✎	blue
✎	turquoise
✎	tan
✎	brown
✎	dk grey

EMBROIDERY FLOSS

✎	dk grey - 3 strands
✎	dk grey - 6 strands
●	white French Knot - 2 strands

Right Arm (20 x 14 threads)

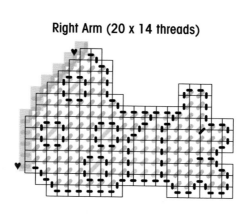

Left Arm (20 x 14 threads)

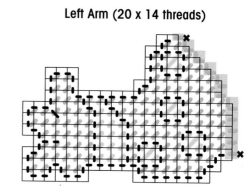

Right Leg (29 x 24 threads)

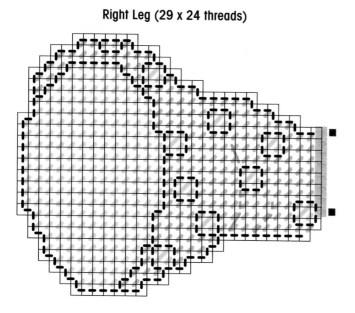

Left Leg (29 x 24 threads)

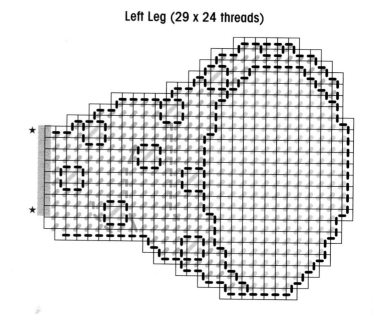

Body (38 x 71 threads)

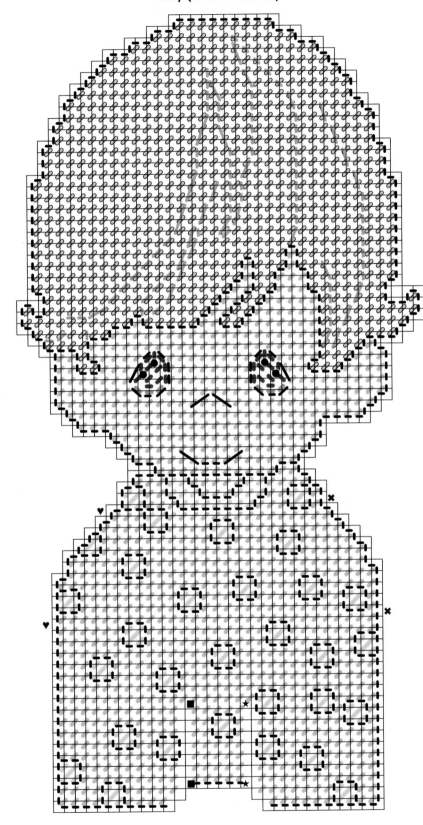

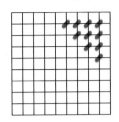

Small Block Top/Bottom

(10 x 10 threads) (stitch 2)

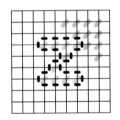

Small Block Side #1

(10 x 10 threads) (stitch 2)

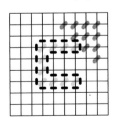

Small Block Side #2

(10 x 10 threads) (stitch 2)

Continued on page 46

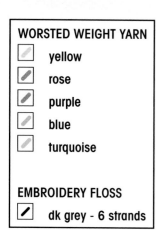

WORSTED WEIGHT YARN

- ▨ yellow
- ▨ rose
- ▨ purple
- ▨ blue
- ▨ turquoise

EMBROIDERY FLOSS

- ✎ dk grey - 6 strands

"B" Block Side (21 x 21 threads) (stitch 8)

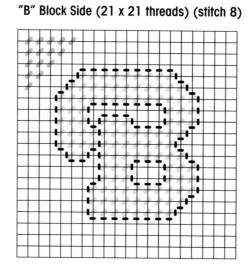

"B" Block Top/Bottom (21 x 21 threads) (stitch ◀

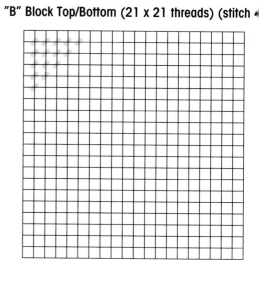

"A" Block Side (21 x 21 threads) (stitch 4)

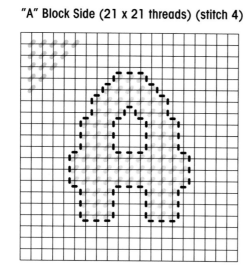

"A" Block Top/Bottom (21 x 21 threads) (stitch 2)

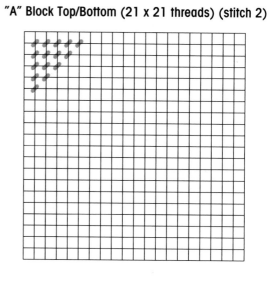

"Y" Block Side (21 x 21 threads) (stitch 4)

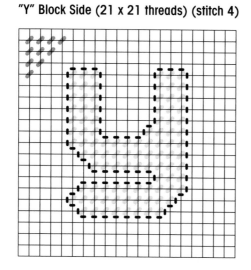

"Y" Block Top/Bottom (21 x 21 threads) (stitch 2)

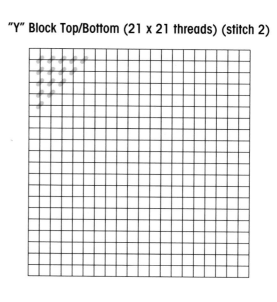

Charming Totes

(Shown on page 9)

Size: 10½"w x 15"h x 3¾"d

Supplies for One Tote Bag: Worsted weight yarn, embroidery floss, three 12" x 18" sheets of clear 7 mesh plastic canvas, and #16 tapestry needle

Stitches Used: Backstitch, French Knot, Gobelin Stitch, Overcast Stitch, and Tent Stitch

Instructions: Follow charts to cut and stitch pieces for desired Tote Bag. Before adding Backstitches, complete background of Front with white Tent Stitches as indicated on chart.

For Back, cut a piece of plastic canvas 71 x 65 threads. For Bottom, cut a piece of plastic canvas 25 x 71 threads. Using matching color yarn, cover unworked pieces with Gobelin Stitches worked over three threads (see Side).

Join Front to Sides. Join Back to Sides. Join Bottom to Front, Back, and Sides. Cover unworked edges of Back. Securely tack Handles to Tote Bag.

WORSTED WEIGHT YARN	
⬛	boy - turquoise
	girl - purple

Handle

(6 x 107 threads)

(stitch 2)

Side (25 x 65 threads) (stitch 2)

Continued on page 48

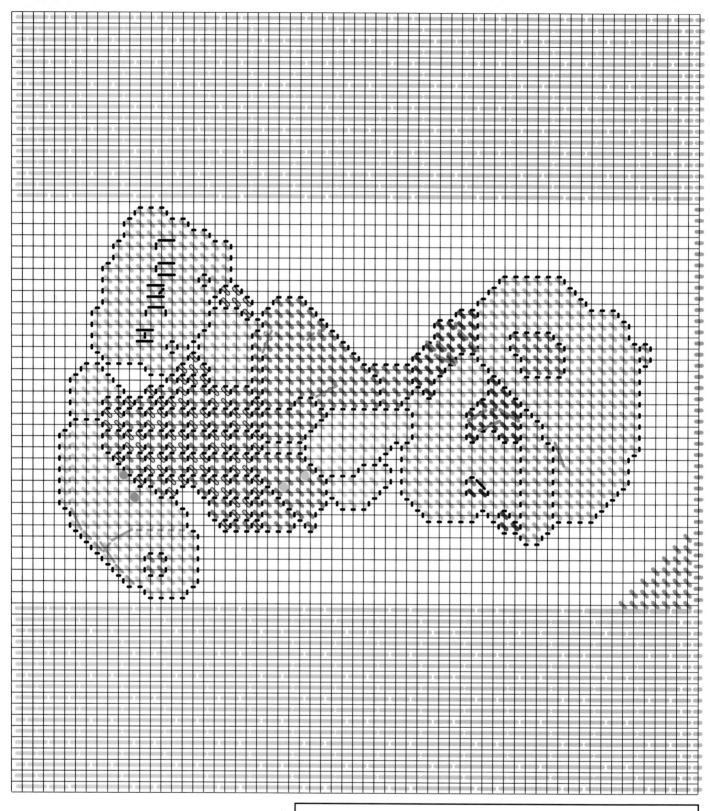

WORSTED WEIGHT YARN

▨	white
▨	yellow
▨	flesh
▨	gold
▨	rose
▨	blue
▨	turquoise
▨	green
▨	tan
▨	brown
▨	dk grey
●	purple French Knot
●	turquoise French Knot

EMBROIDERY FLOSS

╲	dk grey - 3 strands
╲	dk grey - 6 strands

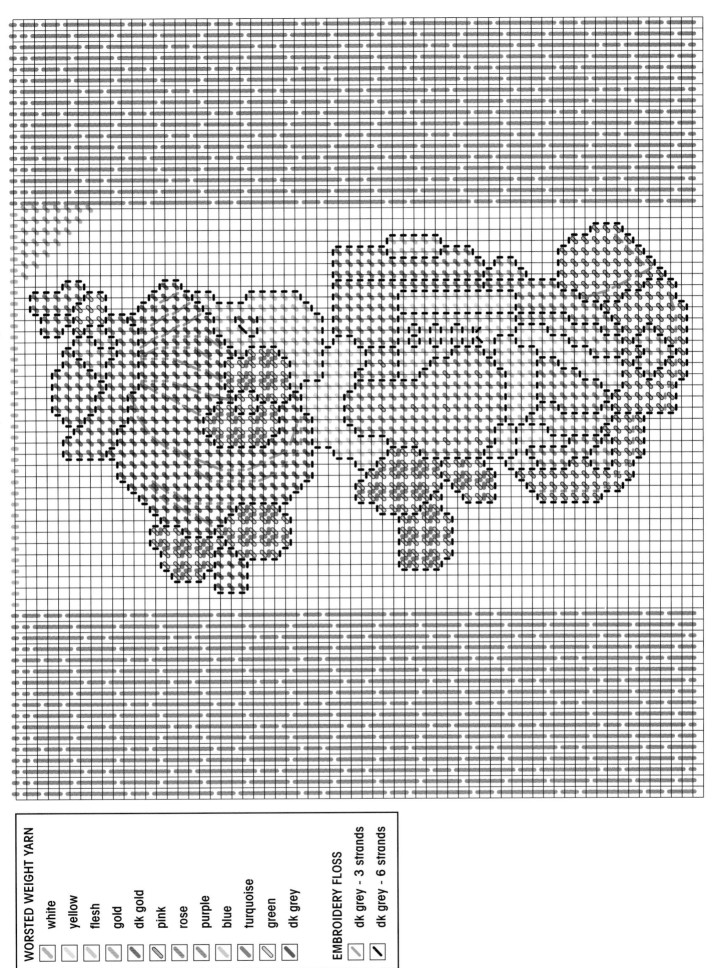

Girl Front (71 x 65 threads)

WORSTED WEIGHT YARN

white
yellow
flesh
gold
dk gold
pink
rose
purple
blue
turquoise
green
dk grey

EMBROIDERY FLOSS

dk grey - 3 strands
dk grey - 6 strands

Teacher (34 x 64 threads)

Terrific Teacher Tissue Cover

(Shown on page 11)

Size: 5³/₄"w x 6¹/₄"h x 4³/₄"d
(Fits a 4¹/₄"w x 5³/₈"h x 4¹/₄"d boutique tissue box.)

Supplies: Sport weight yarn, embroidery floss, two 10¹/₂" x 13¹/₂" sheets of clear 10 mesh plastic canvas, one 10¹/₂" x 13¹/₂" sheet of white 10 mesh plastic canvas, #20 tapestry needle, and craft glue

Stitches Used: Alternating Scotch Stitch, Backstitch, French Knot, Overcast Stitch, and Tent Stitch

Instructions: Follow chart to cut and stitch Teacher on white plastic canvas. Follow charts to cut and stitch remaining tissue box cover pieces on clear plastic canvas. Before adding Backstitches, complete background of Front using brown and dk grey Tent Stitches as indicated on chart.

Using brown yarn, match long edges and join Front to Sides. Join Back to Sides. Join Top to Front, Back, and Sides. Glue Girl to tissue box cover.

Top (46 x 46 threads)

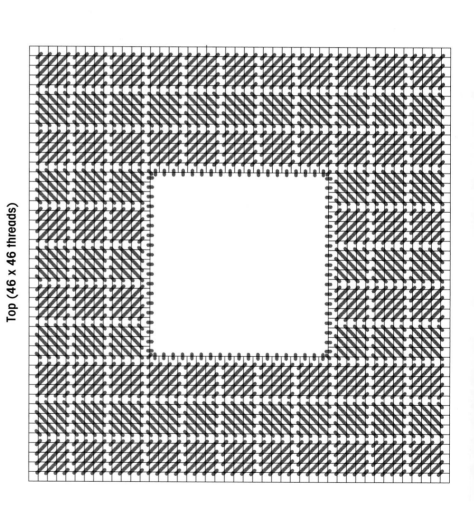

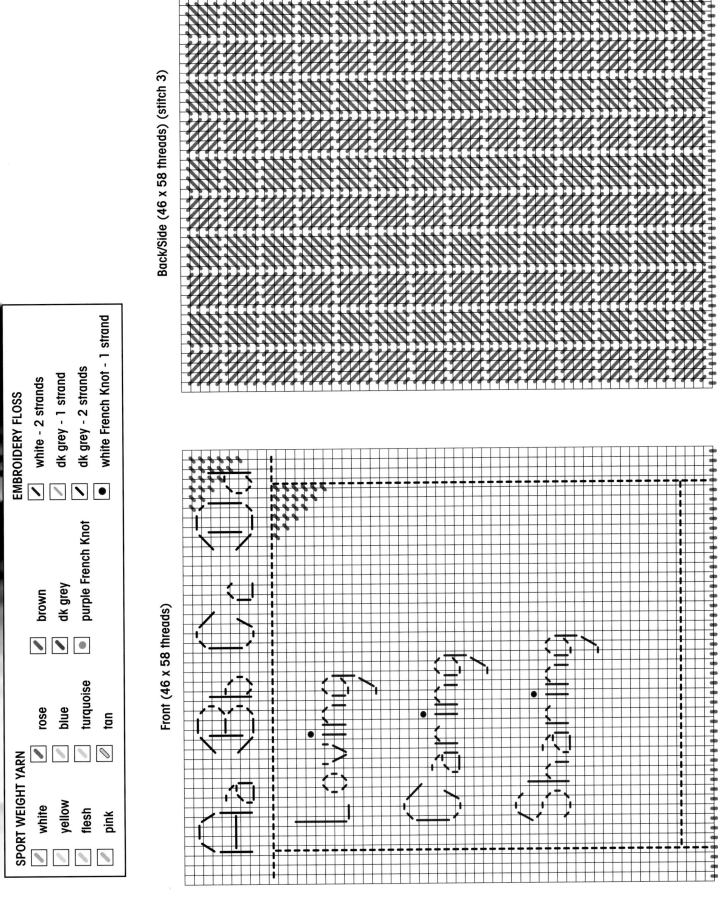

SPORT WEIGHT YARN

	white		rose
	yellow		blue
	flesh		turquoise
	pink		tan

	brown
	dk grey
●	purple French Knot

EMBROIDERY FLOSS

╱	white - 2 strands
╱	dk grey - 1 strand
╱	dk grey - 2 strands
●	white French Knot - 1 strand

Back/Side (46 x 58 threads) (stitch 3)

Front (46 x 58 threads)

Endearing Yuletide Banner

(Shown on page 12)

Size: $11\frac{1}{2}$"w x $10\frac{1}{2}$"h

Supplies: Worsted weight yarn, sport weight yarn, embroidery floss, one $10\frac{1}{2}$" x $13\frac{1}{2}$" sheet of white 7 mesh plastic canvas, one $10\frac{1}{2}$" x $13\frac{1}{2}$" sheet of white 10 mesh plastic canvas, #16 tapestry needle, #20 tapestry needle, $9\frac{1}{2}$" long x $\frac{1}{2}$" diameter dowel rod, two 1" diameter end caps, white paint (optional), and craft glue

Stitches Used: Backstitch, French Knot, Gobelin Stitch, Overcast Stitch, Scotch Stitch, and Tent Stitch

Instructions: Follow chart to cut and stitch Children with Tree on 10 mesh plastic canvas. Follow charts to cut and stitch Banner and Tabs on 7 mesh plastic canvas.

Matching ✖'s and ▲'s, bend Tabs and join to Banner using red yarn. Glue Children with Tree to Banner.

If desired, paint dowel and end caps. Insert dowel through Tabs. Glue end caps to dowel.

Tab (7 x 19 threads)

(stitch 5) 7 mesh

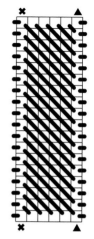

WORSTED WEIGHT YARN	
╱	white
╱	red

Banner (62 x 62 threads) 7 mesh

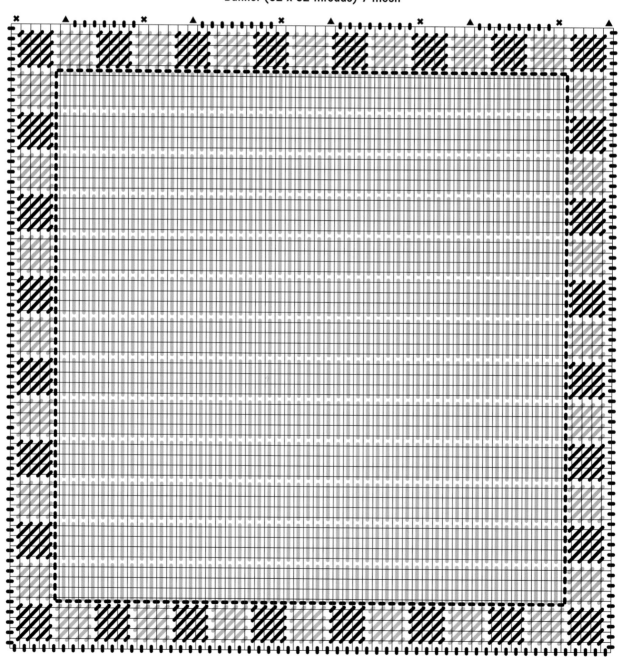

52

SPORT WEIGHT YARN

⬚ white		⬚ blue		
⬚ yellow		⬚ dk green		
⬚ flesh		⬚ tan		
⬚ rose		⬚ brown		
⬚ red		⬚ dk grey		
⬚ purple		⬚ yellow French Knot		

EMBROIDERY FLOSS

⬚ dk grey - 1 strand

⬚ dk grey - 2 strands

Children with Tree (75 x 75 threads) 10 mesh

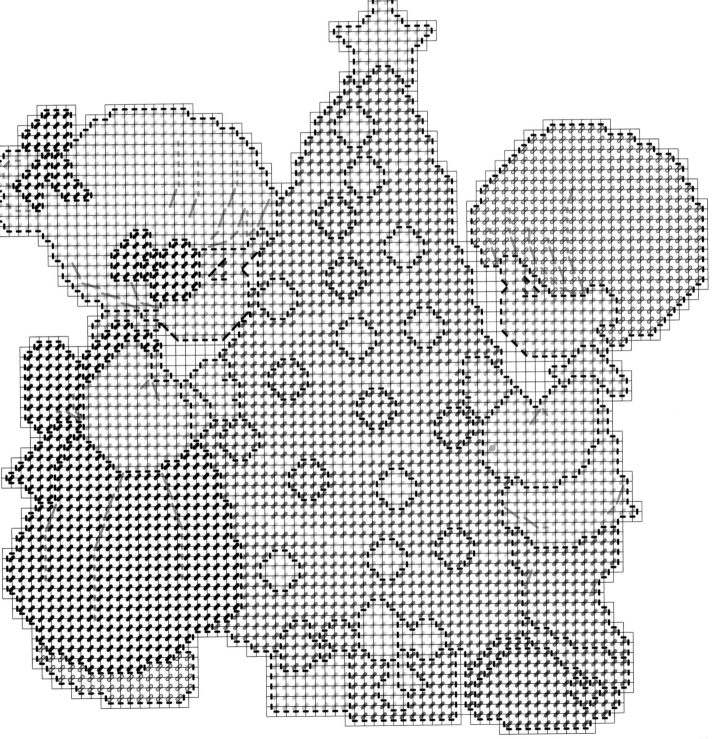

Treasure Box

(Shown on page 14)

Size: 9¹/₂"w x 9¹/₂"h x 3"d

Supplies: Worsted weight yarn, embroidery floss, three 10¹/₂" x 13¹/₂" sheets of clear 7 mesh stiff plastic canvas, #16 tapestry needle, and craft glue

Stitches Used: Alicia Lace Stitch, Backstitch, French Knot, Gobelin Stitch, Lazy Daisy Stitch, Overcast Stitch, and Tent Stitch

Instructions: Follow charts to cut and stitch pieces. Complete background of Top with blue Gobelin Stitches as indicated on chart before adding Backstitches, French Knots, and Lazy Daisy Stitches. Using matching color yarn, cover unworked edges of Fish and Cloud.

Using blue yarn, match short edges and join Top Sides together. Join Top to Top Sides along unworked edges.

For Bottom, cut a piece of canvas 62 x 62 threads. (**Note:** Bottom is not worked.) Match short edges and join Bottom Sides together. Join Bottom to Bottom Sides along unworked edges.

Glue Cloud and Fish to Box.

WORSTED WEIGHT YARN

✏	white
✏	flesh
✏	pink
✏	purple
✏	blue
✏	turquoise
✏	green
✏	tan
✏	brown
✏	grey
✏	dk grey
✏	dk grey - 2-ply
●	rose French Knot
●	purple French Knot
●	blue French Knot
●	green French Knot
●	dk grey French Knot - 2-ply
⊘	yellow Lazy Daisy
⊘	rose Lazy Daisy
⊘	blue Lazy Daisy
⊘	green Lazy Daisy

EMBROIDERY FLOSS

✏	rose - 3 strands
✏	dk grey - 3 strands
✏	dk grey - 6 strands
✏	vy dk grey - 3 strands
●	dk grey French Knot - 3 strands

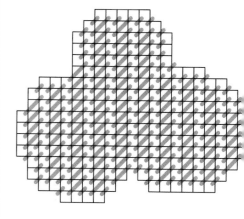

Cloud (22 x 18 threads)

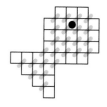

Fish (9 x 9 threads)

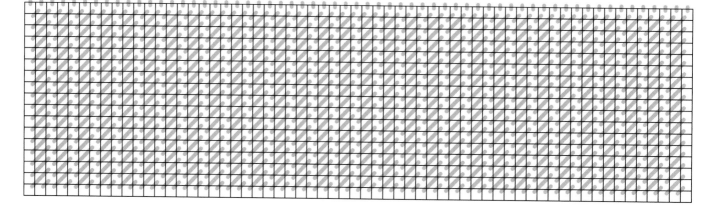

Bottom Side (62 x 18 threads) (stitch 4)

Top Side (64 x 8 threads) (stitch 4)

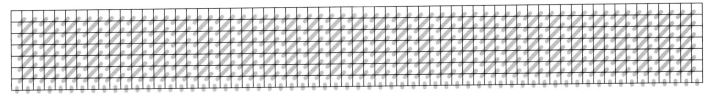

Top (64 x 64 threads)

Tooth Fairy Baskets

(Shown on page 22)

Approx Size: $3^1/_4$"w x $6^3/_4$"h x $1^1/_4$"d each

Supplies for One Basket: Sport weight yarn, embroidery floss, one $10^1/_2$" x $13^1/_2$" sheet of white 10 mesh plastic canvas, and #20 tapestry needle

Stitches Used: Backstitch, Cross Stitch, French Knot, Gobelin Stitch, Lazy Daisy Stitch, Overcast Stitch, and Tent Stitch

Instructions: Follow chart to cut and stitch pieces for desired Basket. For Front, complete background using white Tent Stitches as indicated on chart before adding words, stems, and leaves. Using white yarn, match ✖'s and join Front to Back. Join Bottom to Front and Back.

Bedtime Prayers

(Shown on page 15)

Supplies for One Framed Piece: Worsted weight yarn, embroidery floss, one $10^1/_2$" x $13^1/_2$" sheet of white 7 mesh plastic canvas, #16 tapestry needle, and custom frame

Stitches Used: Backstitch, Cross Stitch, French Knot, and Tent Stitch

Instructions: Center and stitch design on canvas. Trim canvas to desired size. Insert stitched piece into custom frame.

Girl Back (33 x 69 threads)

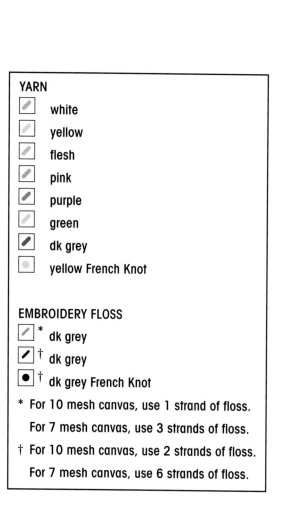

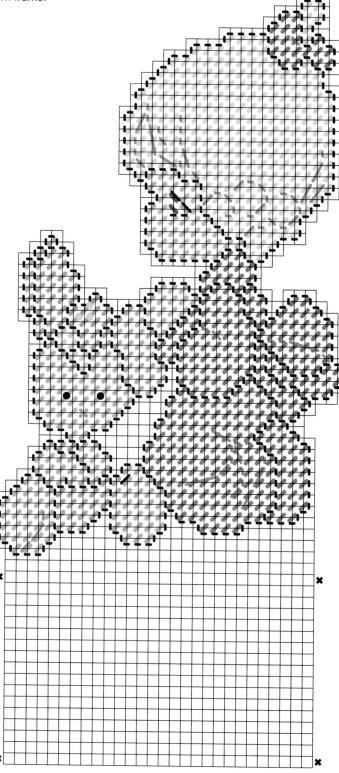

YARN

- white
- yellow
- flesh
- pink
- purple
- green
- dk grey
- yellow French Knot

EMBROIDERY FLOSS

- * dk grey
- † dk grey
- ● † dk grey French Knot

* For 10 mesh canvas, use 1 strand of floss.

  For 7 mesh canvas, use 3 strands of floss.

† For 10 mesh canvas, use 2 strands of floss.

  For 7 mesh canvas, use 6 strands of floss.

56

Front (43 x 18 threads)

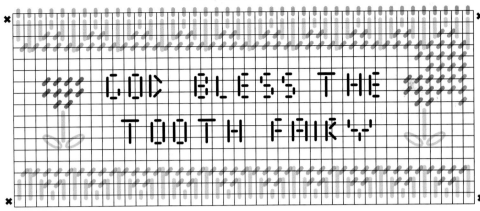

GOD BLESS THE
TOOTH FAIRY

Boy Back (34 x 67 threads)

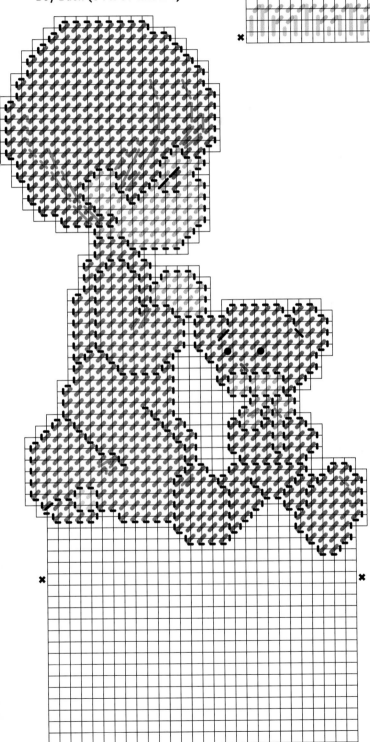

YARN

- white
- yellow
- flesh
- pink
- purple
- green
- brown
- dk grey
- green Lazy Daisy

EMBROIDERY FLOSS

- / * dk grey
- / † dk grey
- ● † dk grey French Knot

* For 10 mesh canvas, use 1 strand of floss.

For 7 mesh canvas, use 3 strands of floss.

† For 10 mesh canvas, use 2 strands of floss.

For 7 mesh canvas, use 6 strands of floss.

Bottom (29 x 14 threads)

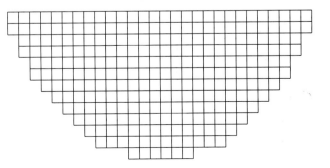

Rainy Day Bank
(Shown on page 17)

Size: 4³/₄"w x 7³/₄"h x 1³/₄"d

Supplies: Worsted weight yarn, sport weight yarn, embroidery floss, one 10¹/₂" x 13¹/₂" sheet of clear 7 mesh plastic canvas, one 10¹/₂" x 13¹/₂" sheet of white 10 mesh plastic canvas, #16 tapestry needle, #20 tapestry needle, and craft glue

Stitches Used: Backstitch, French Knot, Gobelin Stitch, Overcast Stitch, and Tent Stitch

Instructions: Follow chart to cut and stitch Girl on 10 mesh plastic canvas. Follow charts to cut and stitch remaining Bank pieces on 7 mesh plastic canvas.

Using yellow yarn, match long edges and join Front to Sides. Join Back to Sides. Join Bottom to Front, Back, and Sides. Join Top to Front, Back, and Sides. Glue Girl to Bank.

Girl (42 x 78 threads) 10 mesh

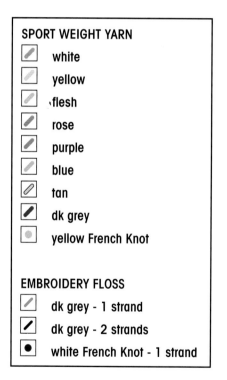

	SPORT WEIGHT YARN
⬜	white
⬜	yellow
⬜	flesh
⬜	rose
⬜	purple
⬜	blue
⬜	tan
⬛	dk grey
●	yellow French Knot

	EMBROIDERY FLOSS
⬜	dk grey - 1 strand
⬜	dk grey - 2 strands
●	white French Knot - 1 strand

WORSTED WEIGHT YARN

✏️ yellow

▨ green

⬤ rose French Knot

Top (32 x 11 threads) 7 mesh

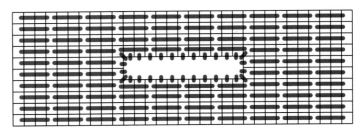

Front/Back (32 x 36 threads) (stitch 2) 7 mesh

Side (11 x 36 threads)
(stitch 2) 7 mesh

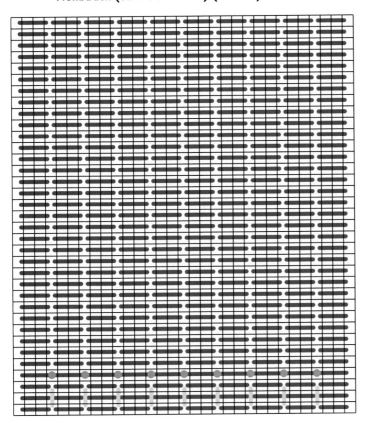

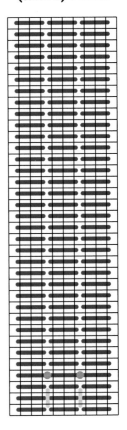

Bottom (32 x 11 threads) 7 mesh

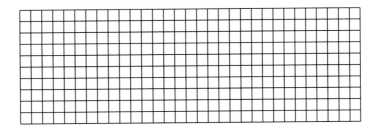

A Stitch In Time Sewing Set

(Shown on page 19)

Needle Case Size: 4$\frac{1}{2}$"w x 3$\frac{1}{2}$"h x $\frac{1}{2}$"d
Chatelaine Size: 40$\frac{1}{2}$"l
Box Size: 13"w x 13"h x 7$\frac{1}{2}$"d
Supplies: Worsted weight yarn, embroidery floss, one 10$\frac{1}{2}$" x 13$\frac{1}{2}$" sheet of clear 7 mesh plastic canvas, one 10$\frac{1}{2}$" x 13$\frac{1}{2}$" sheet of white 7 mesh plastic canvas, #16 tapestry needle, 2$\frac{1}{4}$ yds of $\frac{3}{8}$"w lavender picot-edge satin ribbon, two 3" x 4$\frac{1}{4}$" pieces of white felt, 13"w x 13"h x 7$\frac{1}{2}$"d box, fabric to cover box, ribbon and lace to cover sides of box top, and craft glue

Stitches Used: Backstitch, Cross Stitch, French Knot, Gobelin Stitch, Overcast Stitch, and Tent Stitch
Instructions: Follow chart to cut and stitch Seamstress on white plastic canvas. Follow charts to cut and stitch remaining pieces on clear plastic canvas. For Needle Case Front, complete background with white Tent Stitches as indicated on chart before adding Backstitches.

For Needle Case, join Front to Hinge using white yarn. Join Hinge to Back. To line Needle Case, glue felt to inside of Front and Back pieces.

For chatelaine, knot center of ribbon around scissors handle. Glue ribbon ends to back of Spool.

For box, cover box with fabric. Glue ribbon and lace around sides of box top. Glue Seamstress to top of box.

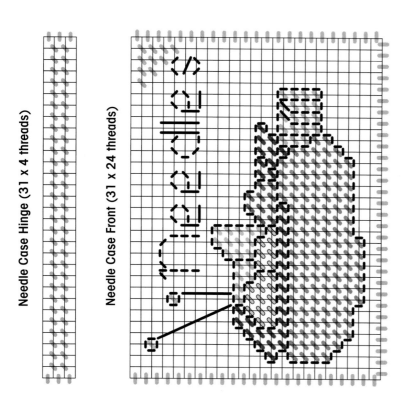

Needle Case Hinge (31 x 4 threads)

Needle Case Front (31 x 24 threads)

Needle Case Back (31 x 24 threads)

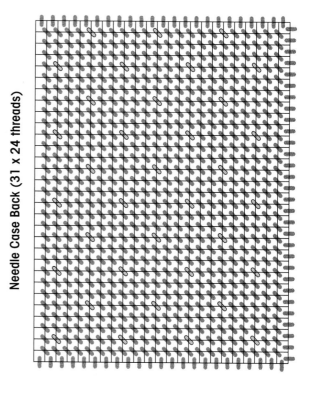

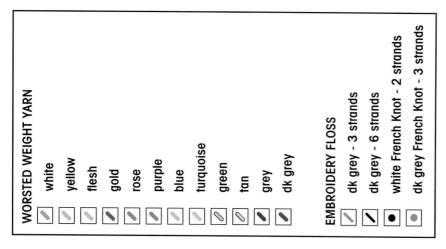

WORSTED WEIGHT YARN

white
yellow
flesh
gold
rose
purple
blue
turquoise
green
tan
grey
dk grey

EMBROIDERY FLOSS

dk grey - 3 strands
dk grey - 6 strands
white French Knot - 2 strands
dk grey French Knot - 3 strands

Spool (13 x 17 threads)

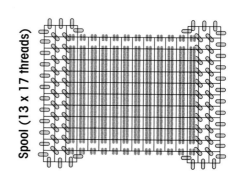

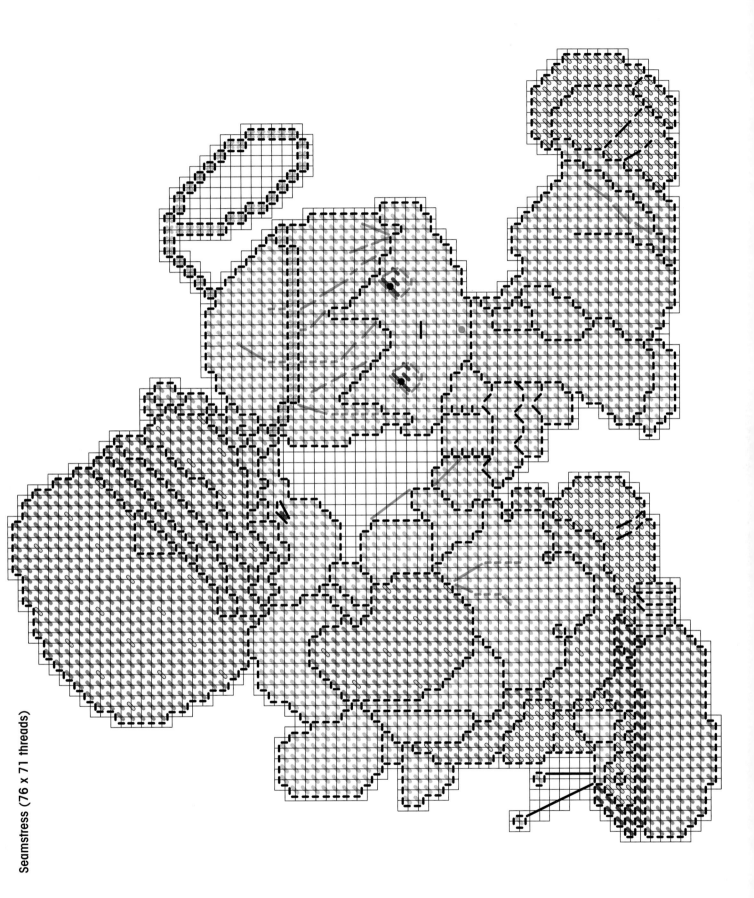

Seamstress (76 x 71 threads)

Blissful Wedding Day Ensemble

(Shown on pages 20 and 21)
Bride and Groom Size: 7$\frac{1}{4}$"w x 8$\frac{1}{4}$"h
Sign Size: 8"w x 2"h
Party Favor Size: 8$\frac{1}{2}$"w x 2"h x 1$\frac{1}{2}$"d

PHOTO ALBUM

Supplies: Sport weight yarn, metallic yarn, embroidery floss, one 10$\frac{1}{2}$" x 13$\frac{1}{2}$" sheet of white 10 mesh plastic canvas, #20 tapestry needle, 10"w x 11$\frac{1}{2}$"h photo album, one yd of fabric, batting, poster board, two 18" lengths of white sheer ribbon with silver edging, 20" length of pink decorative trim, and craft glue
Stitches Used: Backstitch, French Knot, and Tent Stitch
Instructions: Follow chart to cut and stitch Bride and Groom and Sign. Before adding Backstitches, complete background of Sign with white Tent Stitches. Glue pink trim to Sign. Follow instructions below to cover photo album.
Glue Bride and Groom and Sign to photo album. Tie white ribbons into bows and trim ends. Glue one bow to Sign and one bow to top left corner of photo album.

COVERING A PHOTO ALBUM

(**Note:** The following instructions are for an album with center rings. If using an album with off-center rings, you will need to measure each inside cover of album to determine the correct measurements. Use hot glue when covering album.)

1. Remove pages from album.
2. Cut two 3"w fabric strips the height of the album. On the inside of the album, glue one long edge of each strip $\frac{1}{4}$" under each side of rings. Glue remaining edges of fabric strips to album.
3. Cut a piece of batting the same size as the open album. Glue batting to outside of album.
4. Cut a piece of fabric 2" larger on all sides than opened album. Center opened album on wrong side of fabric piece.

5. Fold fabric at top edge of album $\frac{1}{2}$" to wrong side for 2" on each side of center (**Fig. 1**). Insert folded edge of fabric under top edge of rings; glue folded edge of fabric in place. Repeat for bottom edge of album.

Fig. 1

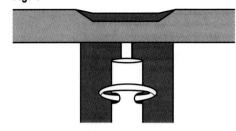

6. Fold each side edge of fabric to inside of album; glue at center only.
7. Making sure fabric on outside of album is smooth and taut, glue remaining edges of fabric to inside of album, folding, pleating, and trimming corners as necessary.
8. To line inside of album, cut two pieces of poster board $\frac{1}{2}$" smaller on all sides than album front. Cut two pieces of fabric 1" larger on all sides than poster board pieces.
9. Center one poster board piece on wrong side of one fabric piece. Fold fabric at corners over edge of poster board; glue in place. Fold remaining fabric edges over edges of poster board; glue in place. Repeat with remaining poster board and fabric.
10. Center and glue one liner, fabric side up, to each inside cover of album.

CENTERPIECE

Supplies: Sport weight yarn, metallic yarn, embroidery floss, one 10$\frac{1}{2}$" x 13$\frac{1}{2}$" sheet of white 10 mesh plastic canvas, #20 tapestry needle, 12" wooden skewer, white paint (optional), and craft glue
Stitches Used: Backstitch, French Knot, and Tent Stitch
Instructions: Follow chart to cut and stitch Bride and Groom. If desired, paint skewer. Glue skewer to back of completed stitched piece. Insert skewer into floral arrangement.

PARTY FAVOR

Supplies for One Favor: Sport weight yarn, one 10$\frac{1}{2}$" x 13$\frac{1}{2}$" sheet of white 10 mesh plastic canvas, #20 tapestry needle, 9"w x 21"l piece of white bridal tulle, two 12" lengths of $\frac{1}{8}$"w rose satin ribbon, two 12" lengths of $\frac{1}{8}$"w white satin ribbon, and candy
Stitch Used: Gobelin Stitch
Instructions: Follow chart to cut and stitch Party Favor. Place a small handful of candy along one short edge of tulle. Roll candy up in tulle and use one color of each ribbon to tie a bow around each end of rolled up tulle. Wrap Party Favor around tulle. Tack corners of Party Favor securely in place.

SPORT WEIGHT YARN	
⟋	white
⟋	pearl metallic
⟋	yellow
⟍	flesh
⟋	rose
⟋	green
⟋	green - 2-ply
⟋	brown
⟋	grey
⟋	dk grey
●	rose French Knot

EMBROIDERY FLOSS	
⟋	dk grey - 1 strand
⟋	dk grey - 2 strands
●	white French Knot - 1 strand

Bride and Groom (75 x 83 threads)

Continued on page 64

Party Favor (30 x 30 threads)

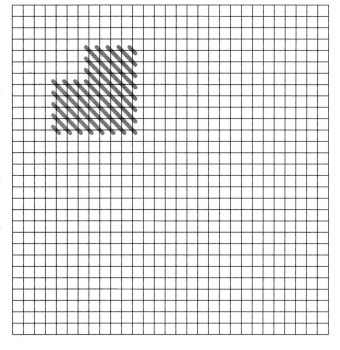

SPORT WEIGHT YARN

white

rose

EMBROIDERY FLOSS

dk grey - 3 strands

Sign (81 x 20 threads)

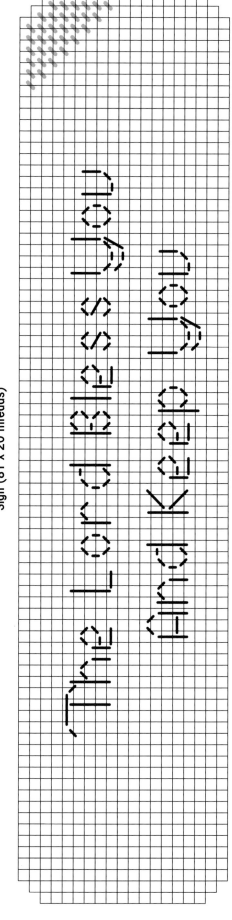

The Lord Bless You And Keep You

Humble Holy Family
(Shown on page 10)

Size: 10¼"w x 8¼"h x 1¾"d

Supplies: Worsted weight yarn, sport weight yarn, embroidery floss, two 10½" x 13½" sheets of clear 7 mesh plastic canvas, one 10½" x 13½" sheet of white 10 mesh plastic canvas, #16 tapestry needle, #20 tapestry needle, sewing needle (for working with nylon thread), nylon thread, and craft glue

Stitches Used: Backstitch, French Knot, Gobelin Stitch, Overcast Stitch, and Tent Stitch

Instructions: Follow chart to cut and stitch Mary and Joseph on 10 mesh plastic canvas. Follow charts to cut and stitch remaining pieces on 7 mesh plastic canvas. Using yellow yarn, cover unworked edges of Star.

To assemble Stable, match ■'s and join Side #1 to Center using tan yarn. Matching ✳'s, join Side #2 to Center. Matching ▲'s and ♥'s, join Bottom to Center and Sides using brown yarn.

Matching ●'s and ★'s, tack Mary and Joseph to Stable Bottom using nylon line. Glue top of Mary and Joseph to Stable Center. Glue Star to Stable.

WORSTED WEIGHT YARN	
╱	tan
╱	brown

Stable Bottom (46 x 46 threads) 7 mesh

Stable Side #1
(15 x 42 threads) 7 mesh

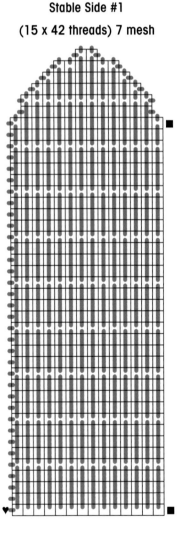

Continued on page 66

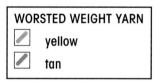

WORSTED WEIGHT YARN

	yellow
	tan

Star
(12 x 12 threads) 7 mesh

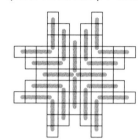

Stable Center (44 x 54 threads) 7 mesh

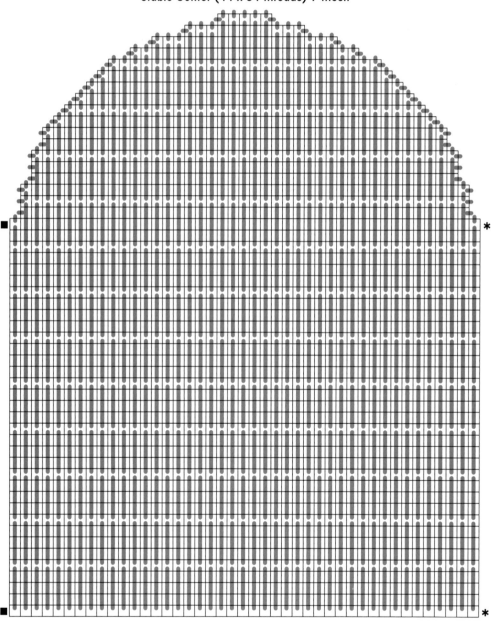

Stable Side #2
(15 x 42 threads) 7 mesh

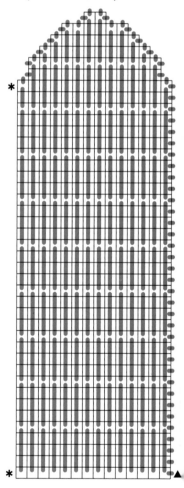

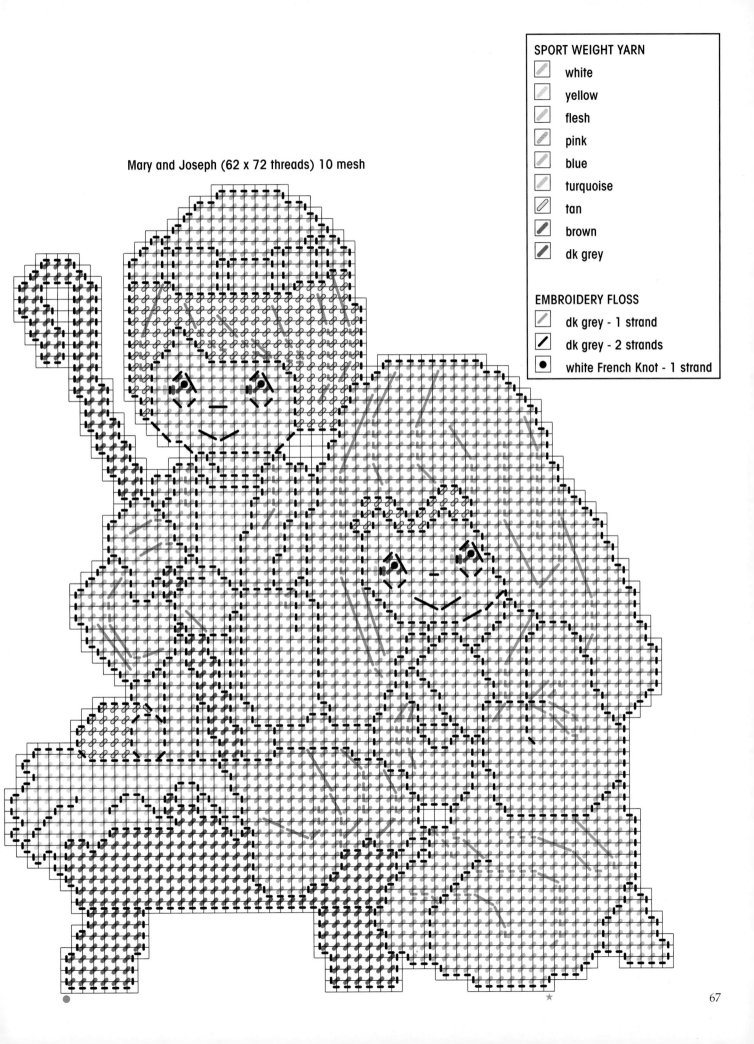

Mary and Joseph (62 x 72 threads) 10 mesh

SPORT WEIGHT YARN

- white
- yellow
- flesh
- pink
- blue
- turquoise
- tan
- brown
- dk grey

EMBROIDERY FLOSS

- dk grey - 1 strand
- dk grey - 2 strands
- white French Knot - 1 strand

Bathing Beauty

(Shown on page 23)

Size: 8"w x 10"h

Supplies: Sport weight yarn, metallic yarn, embroidery floss, one 10½" x 13½" sheet of clear 10 mesh plastic canvas, 8" x 10" frame, and #20 tapestry needle

Stitches Used: Backstitch, French Knot, and Tent Stitch

Instructions: Follow chart to cut and stitch design. Before adding Backstitches, complete background with purple Tent Stitches as indicated on chart. Insert stitched piece into frame.

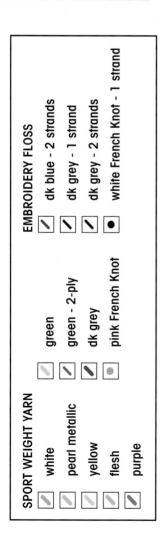

Chart Note: This chart represents one 80 x 100 thread canvas piece. It is spread across two pages to make it large enough to be followed easily. No threads or stitches are repeated from one page to the next.

SPORT WEIGHT YARN

white	
pearl metallic	
yellow	
flesh	
purple	

green	
green - 2-ply	
dk grey	
pink French Knot	

EMBROIDERY FLOSS

dk blue - 2 strands	
dk grey - 1 strand	
dk grey - 2 strands	
white French Knot - 1 strand	

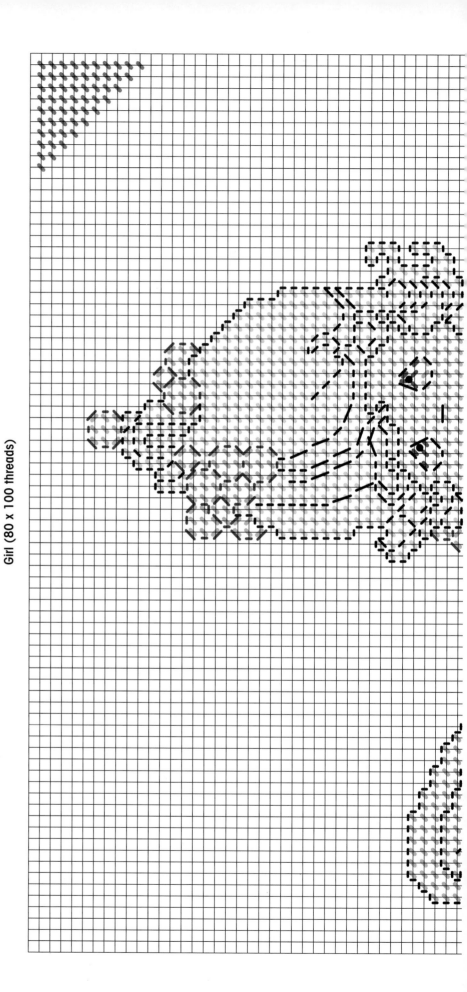

Girl (80 x 100 threads)

Graduate Photo Albums

(Shown on page 24)

Size: 6"w x 4$\frac{3}{4}$"h each

Supplies for One Album: Sport weight yarn, embroidery floss, one 10$\frac{1}{2}$" x 13$\frac{1}{2}$" sheet of clear 10 mesh plastic canvas, #20 tapestry needle, 6$\frac{3}{4}$"w x 5$\frac{1}{2}$"h photo album with $\frac{1}{2}$"w spine, and craft glue

Stitches Used: Backstitch, French Knot, Overcast Stitch, and Tent Stitch

Instructions: Follow chart to cut and stitch desired design. Before adding Backstitches, complete background with Tent Stitches as indicated on chart. Cover unworked edges using matching color yarn. Make tassel using desired color embroidery floss. Glue tassel to stitched piece at ✖. Center and glue stitched piece to album.

SPORT WEIGHT YARN	
⬜	white
⬜	yellow
⬜	flesh
⬜	pink
⬜	purple
⬜	royal blue
⬜	tan
⬜	dk grey

EMBROIDERY FLOSS	
⬜	dk grey - 1 strand
⬜	dk grey - 2 strands
⬤	white French Knot - 1 strand

Girl Graduate (59 x 47 threads)

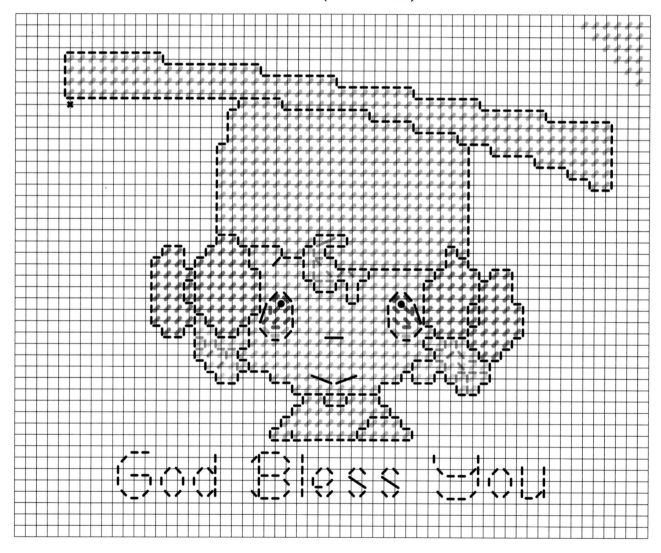

70

HOW TO MAKE A TASSEL

Cut ten 5" lengths and one 20" length of embroidery floss. Fold 5" lengths of floss in half. Make a small loop on one end of 20" length of floss. Refer to **Fig. 1** to wrap 20" length of floss around folded 5" lengths several times, covering almost all of the loop. Thread end of 20" length through loop **(Fig. 2)**. Pull tail of 20" length until loop disappears under wrapped area **(Fig. 3)**. Trim end at top close to wrapped area.

Fig. 1

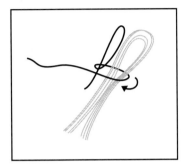

Fig. 2

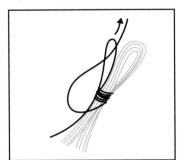

Fig. 3

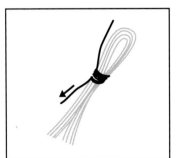

Boy Graduate (59 x 47 threads)

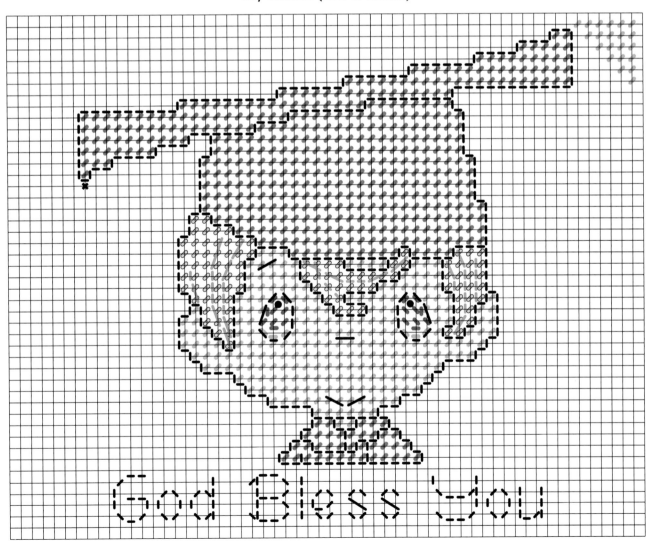

Princely Desk Set

(Shown on page 26)

Pencil Cup Size: $2^3/_4$"w x 4"h x $2^3/_4$"d
Caddy Size: $2^3/_4$"w x $2^1/_4$"h x $2^3/_4$"d
Bookend Size: 5"w x $5^1/_2$"h x 6"d

Supplies: Worsted weight yarn, sport weight yarn, embroidery floss, two $10^1/_2$" x $13^1/_2$" sheets of clear 7 mesh plastic canvas, one $10^1/_2$" x $13^1/_2$" sheet of white 10 mesh plastic canvas, #16 tapestry needle, #20 tapestry needle, $4^3/_4$"w x 5"h x $5^3/_4$"d metal bookend, sewing needle (for working with nylon thread), nylon thread, and craft glue

Stitches Used: Backstitch, French Knot, Gobelin Stitch, Overcast Stitch, and Tent Stitch

Instructions: Follow chart to cut and stitch Prince on 10 mesh plastic canvas. Follow charts to cut and stitch remaining pieces on 7 mesh plastic canvas, leaving stitches in shaded area unworked.

For Pencil Cup, match long edges of Side pieces and join together using white yarn. Join Bottom to Sides.

For Caddy, match short edges of Side pieces and join together using white yarn. Join Bottom to Sides.

For Bookend Cover, cut a 34 x 36 thread piece of 7 mesh plastic canvas for Back (**Note:** Back is not worked.) Work stitches in shaded area to join Front to Base. Join Front to Back along unworked edges of Front. Slide Bookend Cover pieces over metal bookend. Using nylon line, tack bottom of Prince to Bookend Cover. Glue top of Prince to Bookend Cover.

SPORT WEIGHT YARN

- white
- yellow
- flesh
- gold
- purple
- blue
- green
- tan
- dk grey
- blue French Knot

EMBROIDERY FLOSS

- dk grey - 1 strand
- dk grey - 2 strands
- white French Knot - 1 strand

Prince (42 x 51 threads) 10 mesh

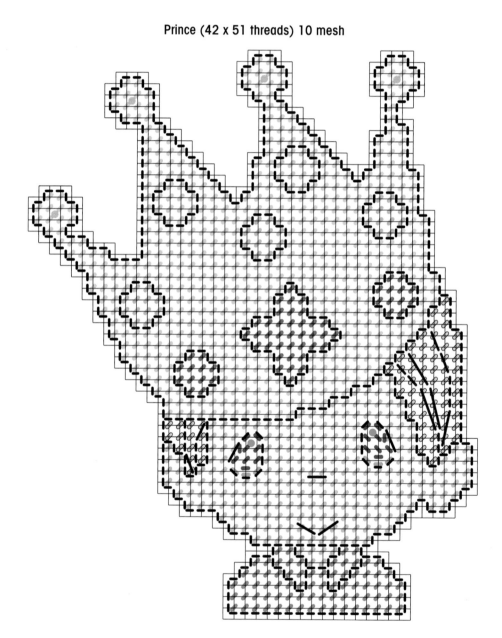

WORSTED WEIGHT YARN
- white - 1 strand
- white - 2 strands
- green - 2 strands

Pencil Cup Side
(18 x 27 threads) (stitch 4) 7 mesh

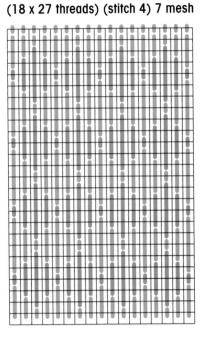

Bookend Cover Front (34 x 36 threads) 7 mesh

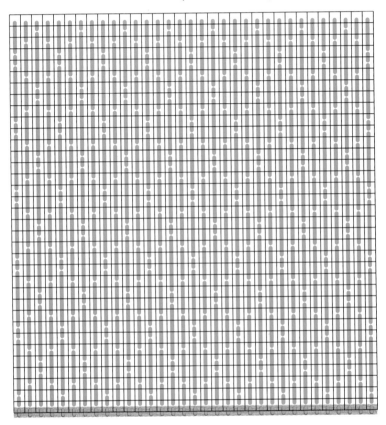

Caddy Side
(18 x 15 threads) (stitch 4) 7 mesh

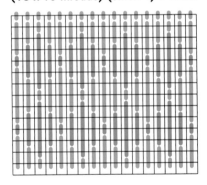

Bookend Cover Base (34 x 15 threads) 7 mesh

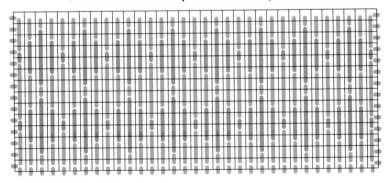

Pencil Cup/Caddy Bottom
(18 x 18 threads) (stitch 2) 7 mesh

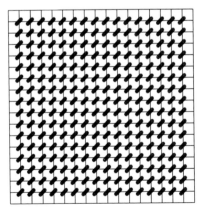

"Jesus Loves Me" Frame

(Shown on page 27)
Size: 13^3/$_4$"w x 8^3/$_4$"h
(**Note:** Photo opening is 4"w x 3^1/$_2$"h)
Supplies: Worsted weight yarn, embroidery floss, one 10^1/$_2$" x 13^1/$_2$" sheet of white 7 mesh plastic canvas, #16 tapestry needle, two sawtooth hangers, and craft glue
Stitches Used: Backstitch, French Knot, and Tent Stitch
Instructions: Follow chart to center and stitch design on canvas, then trim canvas as shown on chart. Glue sawtooth hangers to back of completed stitched piece.

Chart Note: This chart represents one design to be worked on a single sheet of canvas. It is spread across two pages to make it large enough to be followed easily. No threads or stitches are repeated from one page to the next.

WORSTED WEIGHT YARN

- white
- yellow
- gold
- pink
- purple
- blue
- turquoise
- green
- tan
- brown
- dk grey

EMBROIDERY FLOSS

- dk grey - 3 strands
- dk grey - 6 strands
- white French Knot - 2 strands
- dk grey French Knot - 6 strands

"Jesus Loves Me" Frame (91 x 58 threads)
Center and stitch design on canvas, then trim canvas as shown on chart.

Heavenly Inspiration

(Shown on page 28)

Size: 8"w x 10"h

Supplies: Sport weight yarn, embroidery floss, one 10½" x 13½" sheet of clear 10 mesh plastic canvas, 8" x 10" frame, and #20 tapestry needle

Stitches Used: Backstitch, French Knot, and Tent Stitch

Instructions: Follow chart to cut and stitch design. Before adding Backstitches, complete background with blue Tent Stitches as indicated on chart. Insert stitched piece into frame.

Chart Note: This chart represents one 80 x 100 thread canvas piece. It is spread across two pages to make it large enough to be followed easily. No threads or stitches are repeated from one page to the next.

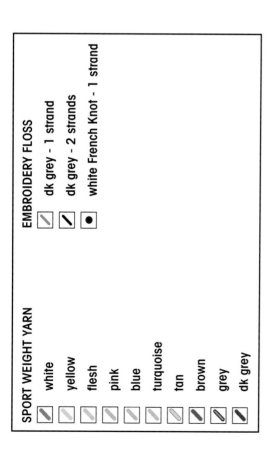

Angels on Cloud (80 x 100 threads)

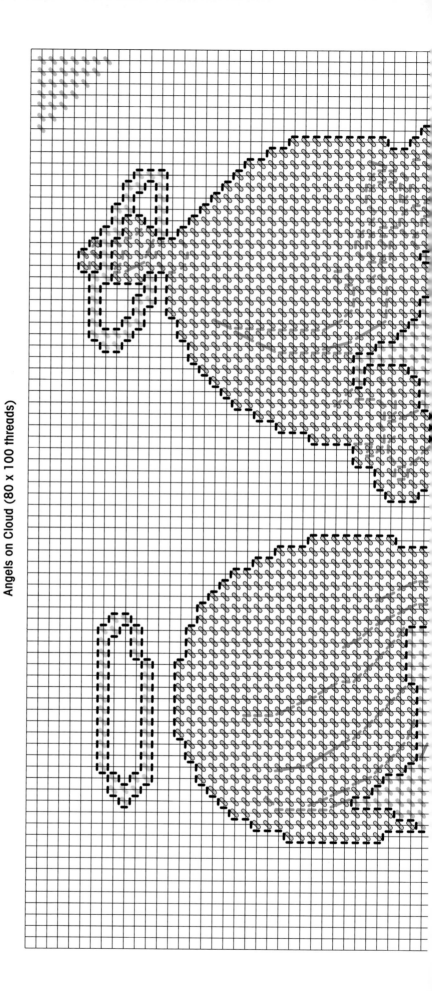

Blessed Bookends

(Shown on page 25)

Approx Size: 7"w x 10½"h x 2½"d each

Supplies for One Bookend: Worsted weight yarn, embroidery floss, two 10½" x 13½" sheets of clear 7 mesh plastic canvas, 3½"w x 7½"h x 2⅛"d brick, plastic wrap, and #16 tapestry needle

Stitches Used: Backstitch, French Knot, Gobelin Stitch, Overcast Stitch, and Tent Stitch

Instructions: Follow charts to cut and stitch pieces for desired Bookend. Using yarn color to match Front, join Front to Sides along unworked edges of Front. Using blue yarn, match long edges and join Back to Sides. Join Top to Front, Back, and Sides along unworked edges. Wrap plastic wrap around brick and insert brick into Bookend. Using matching color yarn, join Bottom to Front, Back, and Sides. Tack loose edges of Front to Top and Sides.

Girl Front (46 x 71 threads)

WORSTED WEIGHT YARN

- white
- yellow
- flesh
- gold
- pink
- rose
- purple
- blue
- turquoise
- green
- brown
- dk grey
- white French Knot
- yellow French Knot

EMBROIDERY FLOSS

- dk grey - 3 strands
- dk grey - 6 strands

WORSTED WEIGHT YARN

- white
- yellow
- flesh
- gold
- rose
- purple
- blue
- turquoise
- green
- tan
- brown
- dk grey
- ● white French Knot
- ● yellow French Knot

EMBROIDERY FLOSS

- dk grey - 3 strands
- dk grey - 6 strands

Boy Front (48 x 71 threads)

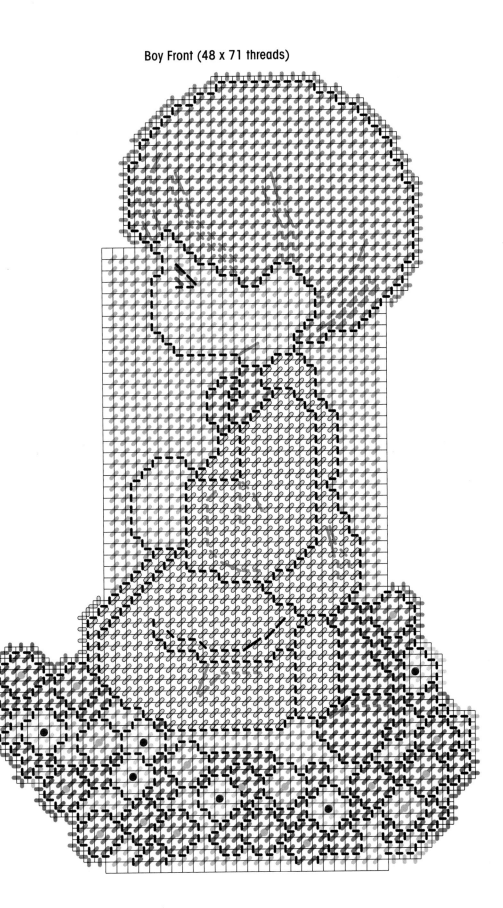

Continued on page 80

Top/Bottom (27 x 17 threads) (stitch 2)

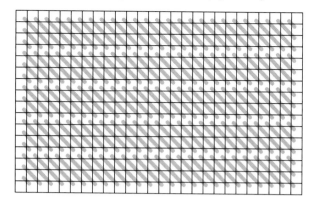

WORSTED WEIGHT YARN

◪ blue

Side (17 x 56 threads) (stitch 2)

Back (27 x 56 threads)

Top/Bottom (27 x 17 threads) (stitch 2)

Country Friends Bookends

(Shown on page 30)

Approx Size: 7½"w x 6½"h x 5¼"d each

Supplies: Worsted weight yarn, sport weight yarn, embroidery floss, two 10½" x 13½" sheets of clear 7 mesh plastic canvas, one 10½" x 13½" sheet of white 10 mesh plastic canvas, #16 tapestry needle, #20 tapestry needle, two 5¾"w x 5"h x 4¾"d metal bookends, sewing needle (for working with nylon thread), nylon thread, and craft glue

Stitches Used: Backstitch, French Knot, Gobelin Stitch, Overcast Stitch, and Tent Stitch

Instructions: Follow chart to cut and stitch Boy and Girl on 10 mesh plastic canvas. Follow charts to cut and stitch remaining pieces on 7 mesh plastic canvas, leaving stitches in shaded area unworked. Before adding French Knots, cover unworked edges of Flower and Leaf pieces using matching color yarn.

For each Bookend Cover, cut a 35 x 34 thread piece of 7 mesh plastic canvas for Back. (**Note:** Back is not worked.) Work stitches in shaded area to join Front to Base. Join Front to Back along unworked edges of Front. Repeat for remaining Bookend Cover. Slide Bookend Cover pieces over metal bookends. Using nylon line, tack Boy and Girl to Bookend Covers. Tack Flower and Leaf pieces to Bookend Covers.

WORSTED WEIGHT YARN	
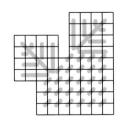 white	
pink	
green	
dk mint green	
● yellow French Knot	

Leaf #1 (5 x 5 threads)

(stitch 2) 7 mesh

Flower #1 (6 x 6 threads)

(stitch 4) 7 mesh

Flower #2 (6 x 6 threads)

(stitch 2) 7 mesh

Bookend Cover Front (35 x 34 threads) (stitch 2) 7 mesh

Leaf #2 (11 x 9 threads)

(stitch 2) 7 mesh

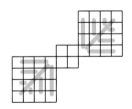

Leaf #3

(10 x 10 threads) 7 mesh

Leaf #4

(10 x 10 threads) 7 mesh

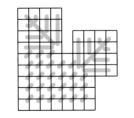

Bookend Cover Base (35 x 21 threads) (stitch 2) 7 mesh

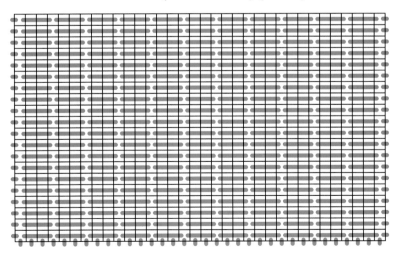

Continued on page 82

Boy (38 x 63 threads) 10 mesh

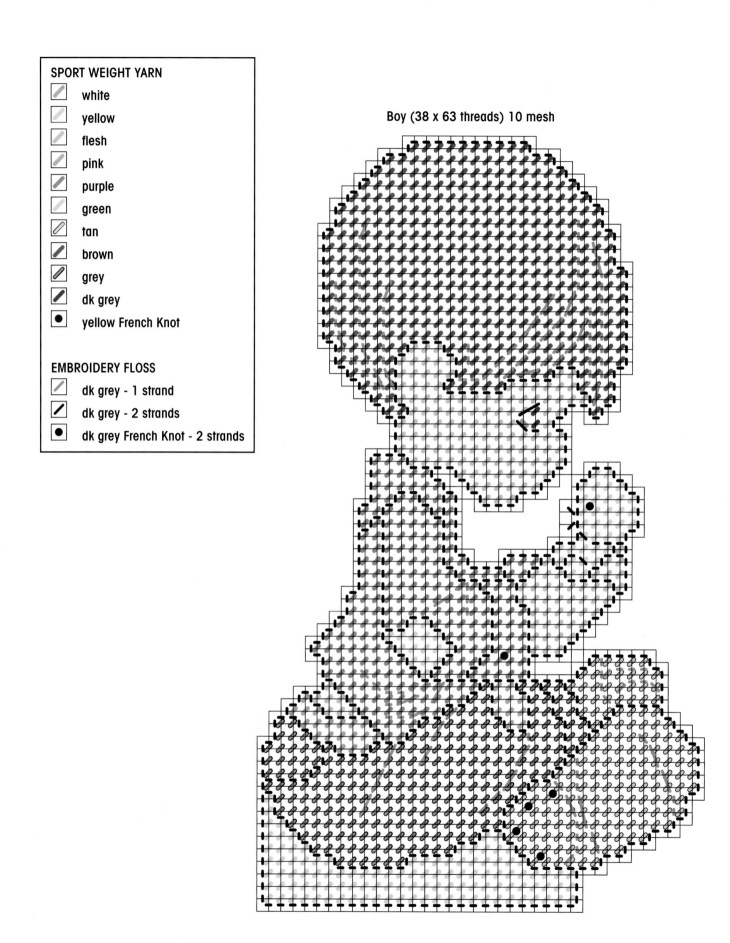

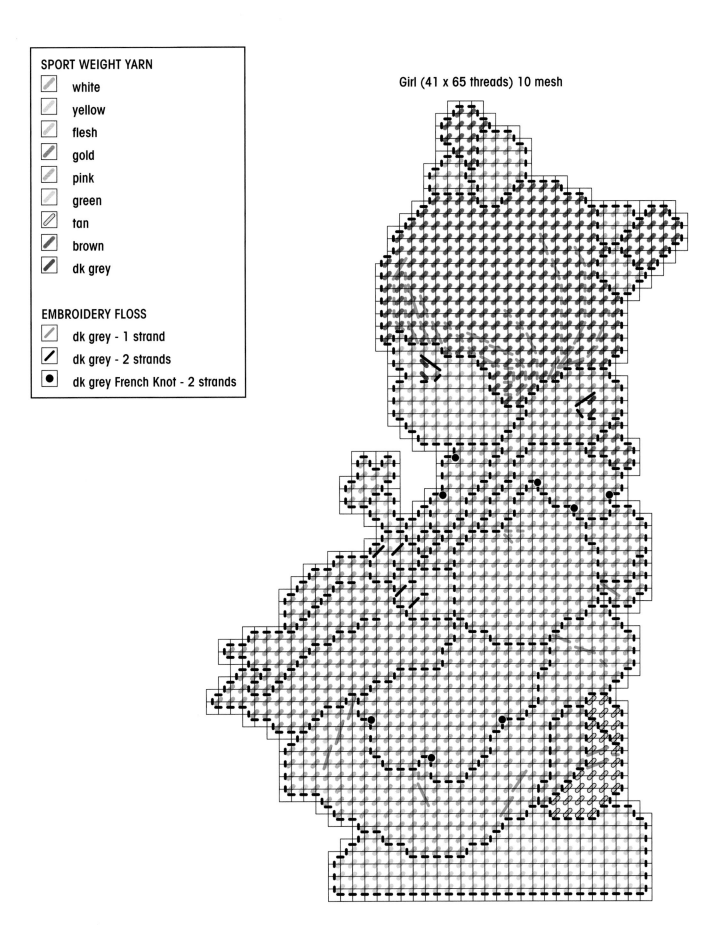

Girl (41 x 65 threads) 10 mesh

SPORT WEIGHT YARN

- white
- yellow
- flesh
- gold
- pink
- green
- tan
- brown
- dk grey

EMBROIDERY FLOSS

- dk grey - 1 strand
- dk grey - 2 strands
- ● dk grey French Knot - 2 strands

Perky Door Decoration

(Shown on page 31)

Size: $17^3/_4$"w x $13^1/_2$"h x $1^1/_4$"d

Supplies: Worsted weight yarn, embroidery floss, two $13^1/_2$" x $21^1/_2$" sheets of clear 5 mesh plastic canvas, #16 tapestry needle, sawtooth hanger, and craft glue

Stitches Used: Alicia Lace Stitch, Backstitch, French Knot, Mosaic Stitch, Overcast Stitch, and Tent Stitch

Instructions: Follow charts to cut and stitch pieces, leaving stitches in shaded area on Bow pieces unworked. Before adding Backstitches and French Knots, cover remaining unworked edges of stitched pieces using two strands of matching color yarn.

Glue Flower and Leaf pieces to Head. Matching ♥'s and ■'s, slide Hat Brim over Head and tack pieces securely together.

Matching ▲'s and ✳'s, bend Bow pieces and work stitches in pink shaded area. Glue Bows to Head.

Matching ◆'s and ✕'s, glue Bodice to back of Head. Glue sawtooth hanger to back of completed stitched piece.

WORSTED WEIGHT YARN - 2 strands		EMBROIDERY FLOSS
white	turquoise	dk grey - 6 strands
flesh	green	dk grey - 9 strands
gold	tan	● white French Knot - 4 strands
pink	brown	
rose	dk grey	
purple	● yellow French Knot	

Head (51 x 55 threads)

Flower #1
(4 x 4 threads)

Flower #2
(4 x 4 threads)

Flower #3
(6 x 6 threads)

Small Leaf
(4 x 4 threads)

Large Leaf
(5 x 5 threads)

Bow (28 x 8 threads) (stitch 2)

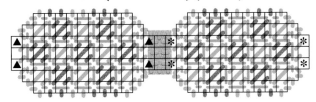

Bodice (31 x 14 threads)

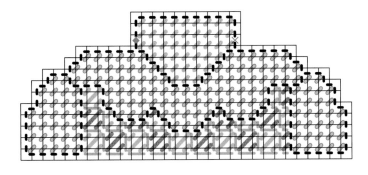

Hat Brim (27 x 87 threads)

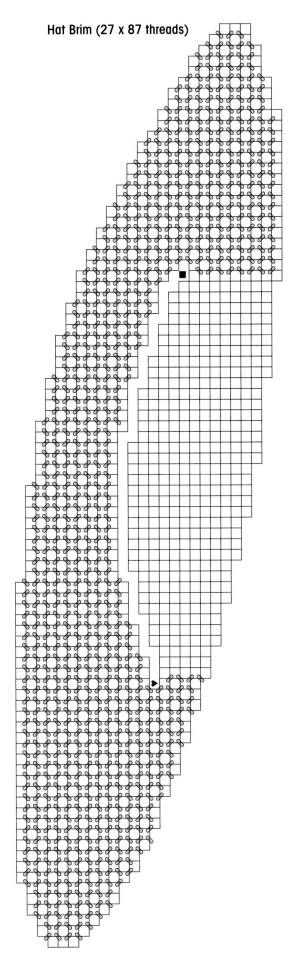

Winsome Door Hanger

(Shown on page 32)

Size: 6½"w x 13½"h

Supplies: Worsted weight yarn, embroidery floss, one 10½" x 13½" sheet of clear 7 mesh plastic canvas, and #16 tapestry needle

Stitches Used: Backstitch, French Knot, Overcast Stitch, and Tent Stitch

Instructions: Follow chart to cut and stitch design. Before adding Backstitches, complete background using blue Tent Stitches as indicated on chart and cover unworked edges using matching color yarn.

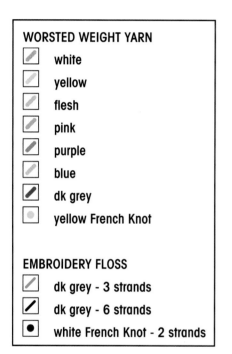

WORSTED WEIGHT YARN

⟋	white
⟋	yellow
⟋	flesh
⟋	pink
⟋	purple
⟋	blue
⟋	dk grey
●	yellow French Knot

EMBROIDERY FLOSS

⟋	dk grey - 3 strands
⟋	dk grey - 6 strands
⦿	white French Knot - 2 strands

Girl (44 x 91 threads)

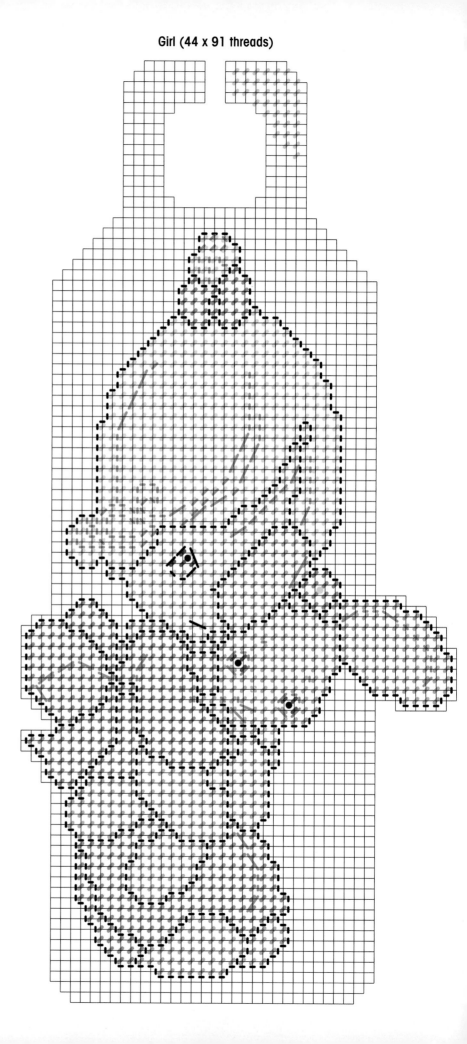

Winsome Door Hanger

(Shown on page 32)

Size: 5"w x 13¹/₂"h

Supplies: Worsted weight yarn, embroidery floss, one 10¹/₂" x 13¹/₂" sheet of clear 7 mesh plastic canvas, and #16 tapestry needle

Stitches Used: Backstitch, French Knot, Overcast Stitch, and Tent Stitch

Instructions: Follow chart to cut and stitch design. Before adding Backstitches, complete background using blue Tent Stitches as indicated on chart. Cover unworked edges using blue yarn.

WORSTED WEIGHT YARN	
▨	white
▨	yellow
▨	flesh
▨	rose
▨	blue
▨	brown
▨	dk grey

EMBROIDERY FLOSS	
▨	dk grey - 3 strands
▨	dk grey - 6 strands
●	white French Knot - 2 strands

Boy (33 x 91 threads)

87

Sweet Dreams Wall Hanging

(Shown on page 33)

Size: 17$\frac{1}{2}$"w x 15$\frac{1}{4}$"h

Supplies: Worsted weight yarn, embroidery floss, one 13$\frac{1}{2}$" x 21$\frac{1}{2}$" sheet of clear 5 mesh plastic canvas, #16 tapestry needle, two sawtooth hangers, and craft glue

Stitches Used: Backstitch, French Knot, Overcast Stitch, and Tent Stitch

Instructions: Follow charts to cut and stitch pieces, leaving stitches in shaded areas unworked. Before adding Backstitches and French Knots, complete backgrounds of stitched pieces with white Tent Stitches as indicated on charts. Match X's and work stitches in shaded areas through both thicknesses of plastic canvas to join Top Section to Bottom Section. Cover unworked edges using two strands of white yarn. Glue sawtooth hangers to back of completed stitched piece.

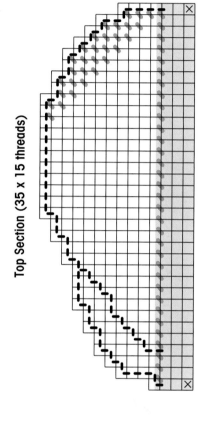

Top Section (35 x 15 threads)

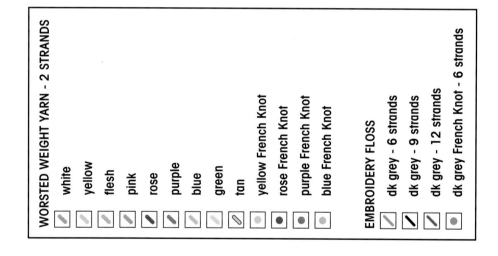

WORSTED WEIGHT YARN - 2 STRANDS	
	white
	yellow
	flesh
	pink
	rose
	purple
	blue
	green
	tan
	yellow French Knot
●	rose French Knot
●	purple French Knot
●	blue French Knot

EMBROIDERY FLOSS	
	dk grey - 6 strands
	dk grey - 9 strands
	dk grey - 12 strands
●	dk grey French Knot - 6 strands

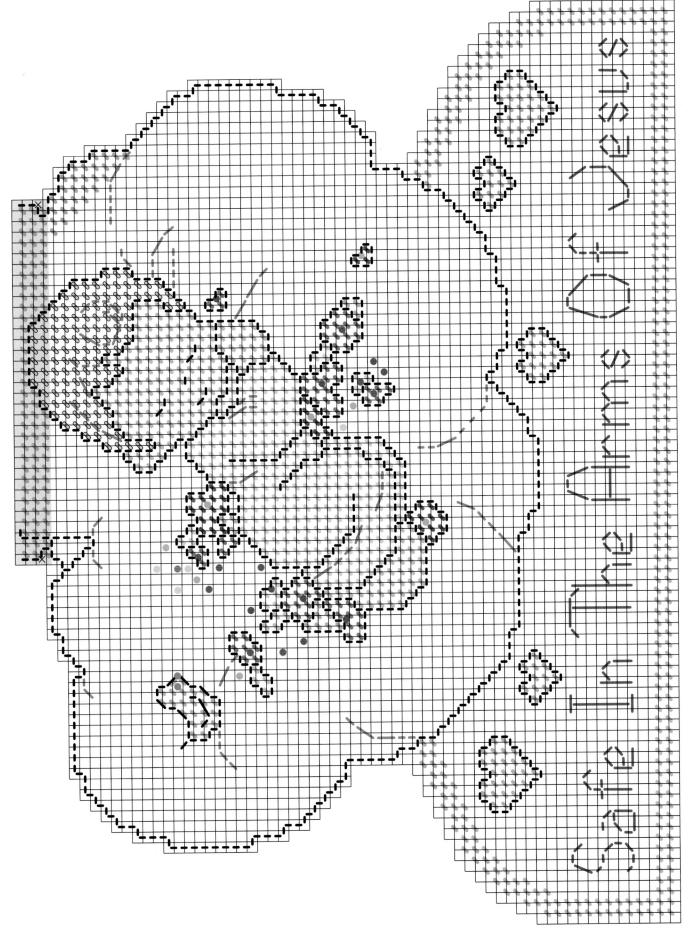

Friends Are Forever Rug

(Shown on page 16)

Size: 22½"w x 19¾"h

Supplies: Worsted weight yarn, embroidery floss, two 13½" x 21½" sheets of clear 5 mesh plastic canvas, #16 tapestry needle, non-skid rug backing (optional), and Scotchgard™ brand fabric protector (optional)

Stitches Used: Backstitch, French Knot, Gobelin Stitch, Mosaic Stitch, Overcast Stitch, and Tent Stitch

Instructions: Follow charts to cut and stitch pieces. Complete background of Girls with white Tent Stitches as indicated on chart. Referring to photo, overlap unworked edges of pieces; using two strands of yellow yarn, baste together through all thicknesses of plastic canvas using a running stitch. Complete borders using Gobelin Stitches. Cover unworked edges of stitched piece. If desired, follow manufacturer's instructions to add backing and fabric protector to Rug.

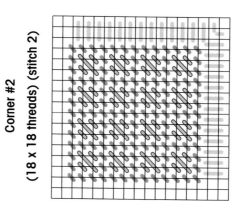

Corner #2
(18 x 18 threads) (stitch 2)

Side Border (67 x 18 threads) (stitch 2)

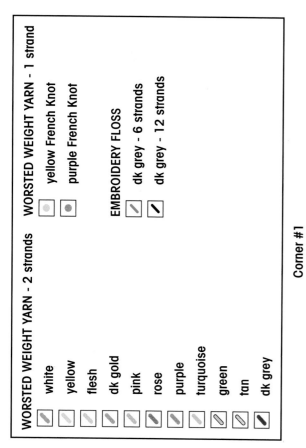

WORSTED WEIGHT YARN - 2 strands

white	
yellow	
flesh	
dk gold	
pink	
rose	
purple	
turquoise	
green	
tan	
dk grey	

WORSTED WEIGHT YARN - 1 strand

yellow French Knot	
purple French Knot	

EMBROIDERY FLOSS

dk grey - 6 strands	
dk grey - 12 strands	

Corner #1
(18 x 18 threads) (stitch 2)

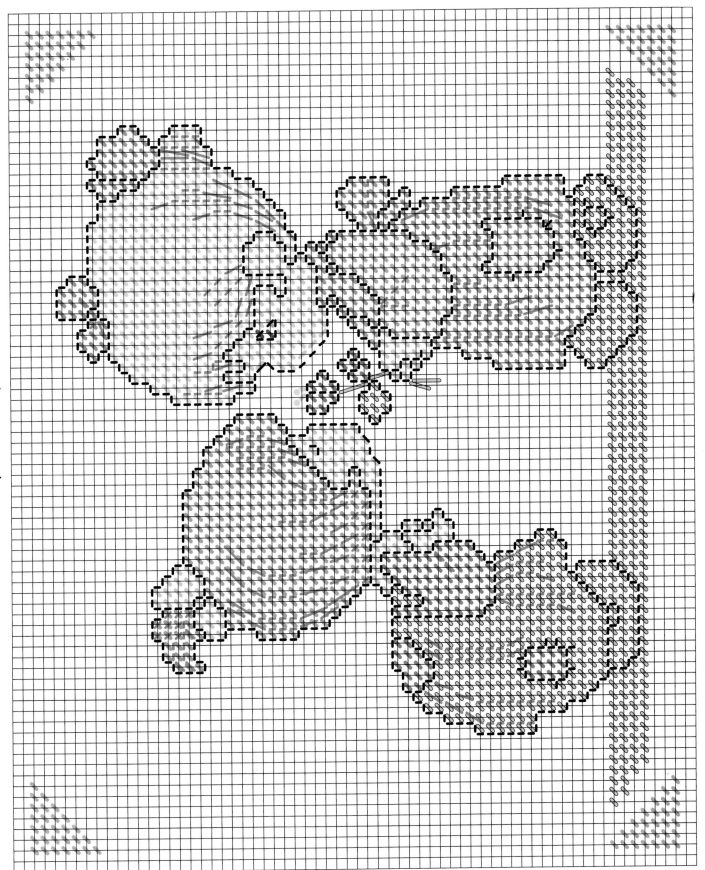

Continued on page 92

WORSTED WEIGHT YARN - 2 strands	
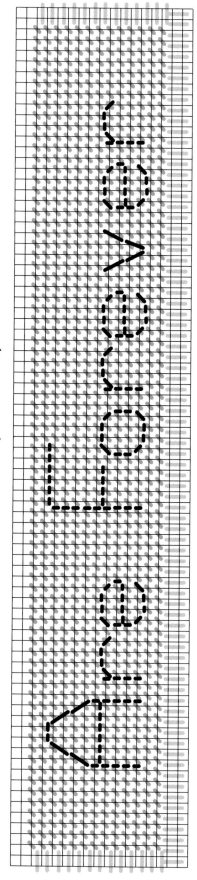	white
	yellow
	grey
	grey French Knot

Top Border (81 x 18 threads)

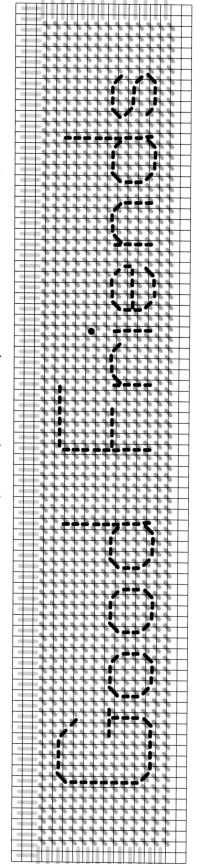

Bottom Border (81 x 18 threads)

GENERAL INSTRUCTIONS

SELECTING PLASTIC CANVAS

Plastic canvas is a molded, nonwoven canvas made from clear or colored plastic. The canvas consists of "threads" and "holes." The threads aren't actually "threads" since the canvas is nonwoven, but it seems to be an accurate description of the straight lines of the canvas. The holes, as you would expect, are the spaces between the threads.

The main difference between types of plastic canvas is the mesh size. Mesh size refers to the number of holes in one inch of canvas. The most common mesh sizes are 5 mesh, 7 mesh, 10 mesh, and 14 mesh. Five mesh means that there are 5 holes in every inch of canvas. Seven mesh canvas is the most popular mesh size.

The project supply list tells you the mesh size, color, and amount of plastic canvas you will need to complete your project.

SELECTING YARN AND EMBROIDERY FLOSS

The projects in this book are made using worsted weight yarn and/or sport weight yarn. Most details are added using embroidery floss. The project instructions will tell you what type of yarn to buy, and the color keys will list the colors needed. If you can't find sport weight yarn in the color needed, worsted weight yarn may be substituted; simply remove one ply of the yarn and stitch with the remaining three plies.

A color palette that duplicates the colors of the Precious Moments® designs is shown on page 34. This palette gives you a sizable, accurate example of each color that was used. When you match your yarn to the colors on the palette, you can be assured that your project will closely resemble the photographed models.

Make sure to buy all of the yarn you need to complete your project from the same dye lot. Although variations in color may be slight when yarns from two different dye lots are held together, the variation is usually apparent on a stitched piece.

SELECTING NEEDLES

Stitching on plastic canvas should be done with a blunt needle called a tapestry needle. The correct size needle to use depends on the canvas mesh size and the yarn thickness (see table for common sizes). The recommended needle size is listed in the supply section of each project.

Mesh	Needle
5	#16 tapestry
7	#16 tapestry
10	#20 tapestry
14	#24 tapestry

WORKING WITH PLASTIC CANVAS

Counting Threads. Throughout this book, the lines of the canvas are referred to as threads. However, they are not actually "threads" since the canvas is not woven. Before cutting out your pieces, note the thread count of each chart. The thread count is listed above the chart and indicates the number of threads in the width and height of the canvas pieces. To cut plastic canvas pieces accurately, count threads (not holes) as shown in **Fig. 1**.

Fig. 1

Marking the Canvas. If you find it necessary to mark on the canvas, use an overhead projector pen. Outline shape with pen, cut out shape, and remove markings with a damp towel.

Cutting the Canvas. When cutting canvas, make sure to cut as close to the thread as possible without cutting into the thread. If you don't cut close enough, "nubs" or "pickets" will be left on the edge of your canvas. Make sure to trim all nubs from the canvas before you begin to stitch, because nubs will snag the yarn and are difficult to cover. A craft knife is helpful when cutting a small area from the center of a larger piece of canvas. When using a craft knife, protect the table below your canvas with a layer of cardboard or a magazine.

WORKING WITH YARN AND FLOSS

Separating Yarn Strands. Most brands of worsted weight yarn have four plies that are twisted together to form one strand. When the instructions indicate "2-ply" yarn, separate the strand of yarn and stitch using only two of the four plies.

Separating Floss Strands. Embroidery floss consists of six strands that are twisted together. To ensure smoother stitches, separate the strands of floss and realign them before threading needle.

READING THE COLOR KEY AND CHART

The color key indicates the colors of yarn used and how each color is represented on the chart. For example, when white yarn is represented by a grey line in the color key, all grey stitches in the chart should be stitched using white yarn.

Whenever possible, the drawing on the chart looks like the completed stitch. For example, the Tent Stitches on the chart are drawn diagonally across one intersection of threads just like Tent Stitches look on your piece of canvas. When a stitch such as a French Knot cannot clearly be drawn on the chart, a symbol will be used instead. If you have difficulty determining how a particular stitch is worked, refer to the Stitch Diagrams, pages 94 and 95.

STITCHING THE DESIGN

Securing the First Stitch. Don't knot the end of your yarn before you begin stitching. Instead, begin each length of yarn by coming up from the wrong side of the canvas and leaving a 1" - 2" tail on the wrong side. Hold this tail against the canvas and work the first few stitches over the tail. When secure, clip the tail close to your stitched piece.

Using Even Tension. Keep your stitching tension consistent, with each stitch lying flat and even on the canvas. Pulling or yanking the yarn causes the tension to be too tight, and you will be able to see through your project. Loose tension is caused by not pulling the yarn firmly enough, and the yarn will not lie flat on the canvas.

Continued on page 94

Ending Your Stitches. After you've completed all of the stitches of one color in an area, end your stitching by running your needle under several stitches on the back of the stitched piece.

JOINING PIECES

Straight Edges. The most common method of assembling stitched pieces is joining two or more pieces of canvas along a straight edge using Overcast Stitches. Place one piece on top of the other with right or wrong sides together. Make sure the edges being joined are even, then stitch the pieces together through all layers.

Shaded Areas. The shaded area is part of a chart that has colored shading on top of it. Shaded areas usually mean that all the stitches in that area are used to join pieces of canvas. Do not work the stitches in a shaded area until your project instructions say you should.

Tacking. To tack pieces, run your needle under the backs of some stitches on one stitched piece to secure the yarn, then run your needle through the canvas or under the stitches on the piece to be tacked in place. The idea is to securely attach your pieces without your tacking stitches showing.

Uneven Edges. Sometimes you'll need to join a diagonal edge to a straight edge. The holes of the two pieces will not line up exactly. Just keep the pieces even and stitch through holes as many times as necessary to completely cover the canvas.

Unworked Threads. Sometimes you'll need to join the edge of one piece to an unworked thread on another piece. Simply place one piece on top of the other, matching the indicated threads or symbols. Join by stitching through both layers.

STITCH DIAGRAMS

> **Unless otherwise indicated, bring threaded needle up at 1 and all odd numbers and down at 2 and all even numbers.**

Alicia Lace Stitch: This series of stitches is worked in diagonal rows and forms a lacy pattern. Follow **Fig. 2** and work in one direction to cover every other diagonal row of intersections, then work in the other direction **(Fig. 3)** to cover the remaining intersections.

Fig. 2

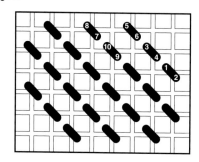

Fig. 3

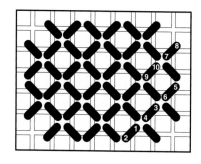

Alternating Scotch Stitch: This Scotch Stitch variation is worked over three or more threads, forming alternating squares as shown in **Fig. 4**.

Fig. 4

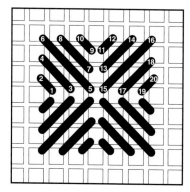

Backstitch: This stitch is worked over completed stitches to outline or define **(Fig. 5)**. It is sometimes worked over more than one thread. Backstitch may also be used to cover canvas as shown in **Fig. 6**.

Fig. 5

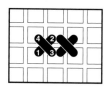

Fig. 6

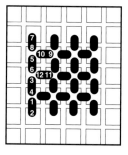

Cross Stitch: This stitch is composed of two stitches **(Fig. 7)**. The top stitch of each cross must always be made in the same direction.

Fig. 7

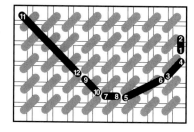

French Knot: Bring needle up through hole. Wrap yarn once around needle and insert needle in same hole or adjacent hole **(Fig. 8)**. Tighten knot, then pull needle through canvas, holding yarn until it must be released.

Fig. 8

Gobelin Stitch: This basic straight stitch is worked over two or more threads or intersections **(Fig. 9)**. The number of threads or intersections may vary according to the chart.

Fig. 9

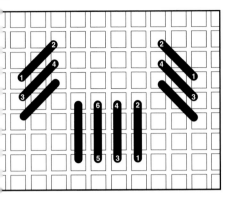

Lazy Daisy Stitch: Bring needle up at 1, make a loop and go down at 1 again **(Fig. 10)**. Come up at 2, keeping yarn below needle's point. Pull needle through and secure loop by bringing yarn over loop and going down at 2.

Fig. 10

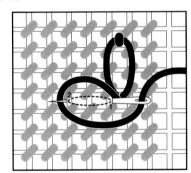

MOSAIC STITCH
This three stitch pattern forms small squares **(Fig. 11)**.

Fig. 11

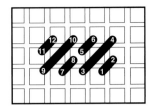

Overcast Stitch: This stitch covers the edge of the canvas and joins pieces of canvas **(Fig. 12)**. It may be necessary to go through the same hole more than once to get even coverage on the edge, especially at the corners.

Fig. 12

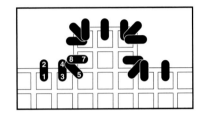

Scotch Stitch: This stitch forms a square. It may be worked over three or more horizontal threads by three or more vertical threads. **Fig. 13** shows it worked over three threads.

Fig. 13

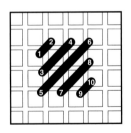

Tent Stitch: This stitch is worked in horizontal or vertical rows over one intersection as shown in **Fig. 14**. Follow **Fig. 15** to work the **Reversed Tent Stitch**. Sometimes when you are working Tent Stitches, the last stitch on the row will look "pulled" on the front of your piece when you are changing directions. To avoid this problem, leave a loop of yarn on the wrong side of the stitched piece after making the last stitch in the row. When making the first stitch in the next row, run your needle through the loop **(Fig. 16)**. Gently pull yarn until all stitches are even.

Fig. 14

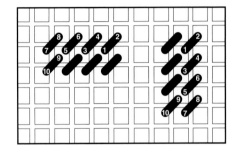

Fig. 15

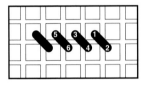

Fig. 16

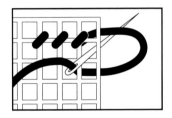

Needlework adaptations by Maryanne Moreck and Teal Lee Elliott.

Instructions tested and photography items made by Janet Akins, Toni Bowden, Kathleen Boyd, Virginia Cates, Juanita Criswell, Sharla Dunigan, Michelle E. Goodrich, Janice Gordon, Vivian M. Heath, Linda Heath, Carlene Hodge, Gary Hutcheson, JoAnne McCallum, Patricia McCauley, Connie McGaughey, Linda Rogers-Peters, George Dudley Shelton, and Sadie Wilson.

INDEX